INTERNATIONAL DEVELOPMENT IN FOCUS

Homes and Hopes

Mobilizing Private Capital for Affordable Housing and Family Investment in Kazakhstan

KATERINA LEVITANSKAYA, MARTIN MELECKY, AND ANDREY MILYUTIN

WORLD BANK GROUP

1 2 3 4   29 28 27 26

ISBN: 978-1-4648-2338-1
ISBN (electronic): 978-1-4648-2339-8
DOI: 10.1596/978-1-4648-2338-1

Cover art: © Duncan Andison / iStock. Used with permission. Further permission required for reuse.
Cover design: Debra Naylor / Naylor Design Inc.

The manufacturer's authorized representative in the European Union for product safety is Mare Nostrum Group B.V., Doelen 72, 4831 GR Breda, The Netherlands. Email: gpsr@mare-nostrum.co.uk.

Homes and Hopes

This book, along with any associated content or subsequent updates, can be accessed at https://hdl.handle.net/10986/44936.

Scan to see all titles in this collection.

Contents

Boxes

Figures

Tables

Preface

This report aims to provide a comprehensive analysis of the Kazakhstani residential mortgage market, including trends, growth determinants, drivers, government policies, market competition, private capital participation, and households' access to mortgage loans. The report is expected to inform the ongoing policy debate on the future direction of mortgage market development by proposing options from the perspective of housing affordability, fiscal efficiency, and private capital mobilization. The aim is to offer actionable insights to stakeholders—policy makers, financial sector authorities, financial institutions, investors, communities, and analysts—to enable informed decision-making and strategic planning.

The analysis is based on public document review and stakeholder interviews, except for the section on corporate governance in chapter 4, which is based solely on the publicly available information. The authors conducted a series of virtual and face-to-face stakeholder interviews from March to September 2025 to gain first-hand information on key sectoral constraints, challenges, and opportunities. Interlocutors included financial sector authorities, public sector institutions, second-tier banks, and industry associations; a complete list is in appendix A. The authors also collaborated with the Agency of the Republic of Kazakhstan for Regulation and Development of the Financial Market in preparing this report.

The scope of the report is limited to the analysis of the residential mortgage market. It does not provide an in-depth review of the housing construction sector or of other aspects of housing supply, development, and financing. However, a comprehensive assessment of these areas is essential for informed housing sector policy discussions and should be undertaken to complement the report's findings and recommendations.

Acknowledgments

This report was prepared by a joint International Finance Corporation (IFC)–World Bank Group team led by Katerina Levitanskaya (senior operations officer, IFC), Martin Melecky (lead economist, World Bank Group), and Andrey Milyutin (consultant, IFC). Team members included Adalyat Abdumanapova (corporate governance officer, IFC), Akbobek Akhmedyarova (researcher, National Analytical Center, Nazarbayev University), Ganbaatar Jambal (senior financial sector specialist, World Bank Group), Oleg Khe (consultant, IFC), Chenyu Mao (economist, World Bank Group), and Maria Turetskaya (senior investment officer, IFC). The report captures the valuable comments and suggestions of the following peer reviewers: Victor Mints (senior operations officer, IFC) and Simon Walley (lead financial sector specialist, World Bank Group).

The team acknowledges the Agency of the Republic of Kazakhstan for Regulation and Development of the Financial Market, the National Bank of Kazakhstan, and the Association of Financiers of Kazakhstan for their productive collaboration with the team as it prepared this report. The team is also grateful to government officials, private sector representatives, and other stakeholders who provided valuable insights that helped improve the quality of the report.

About the Authors and Contributors

ABOUT THE AUTHORS

Katerina Levitanskaya is senior financial sector specialist in the Creating Markets Advisory and Economics Department at the International Finance Corporation (IFC), part of the World Bank Group. She has been working across the World Bank Group on a wide range of financial sector development projects, including analytical and advisory work in the areas of access to finance, housing finance, sustainable finance, financial inclusion, and capital markets in the Europe and Central Asia region. Her engagements include both public sector policy work and development of market-based solutions for private sector clients. Katerina has coauthored policy papers and reports on topics such as micro, small, and medium enterprise access to finance and green finance. Prior to the World Bank, Katerina worked in the financial industry in the United States and the United Kingdom, with her last position as an associate vice president at a structured finance company in New York. A Russian national, Katerina holds a master's degree in international economics from the Russian State University of International Relations and an MBA in finance from HEC Paris in France.

Martin Melecky is lead economist in the Finance, Competitiveness and Innovation Global Practice at the World Bank. He has led financial sector assessment programs, development policy operations, and investment and technical assistance projects in Europe and Central Asia and in South Asia. He has coauthored regional reports, including *Hidden Debt: Solutions to Avert the Next Financial Crisis in South Asia; Economic Corridors in South Asia;* and *Risks and Returns: Managing Financial Trade-Offs for Inclusive Growth in Europe and Central Asia.* He is also the lead author of a chapter in the 2014 *World Development Report* on the role of the financial system in risk management. Martin has published in journals such as the *Cambridge Journal of Regions, Economy and Society;* the *Journal of Banking and Finance;* the *Journal of Financial Stability;* the *Journal of International Money and Finance;*

the *Journal of Regional Science;* the *World Bank Economic Review;* and the *World Bank Research Observer.* A Czech national, he holds a PhD in economics from the University of New South Wales, Australia.

Andrey Milyutin is a global housing finance expert with more than 25 years of international experience in financial sector development, capital markets, and mortgage finance. He is currently housing finance consultant at the World Bank Group, where he advises on strategic sectoral development, refinancing and risk-sharing solutions, legal and regulatory reforms, and capital-market access frameworks. For almost 20 years, he served as senior global housing finance specialist at the World Bank, leading lending and advisory engagements in more than 20 countries across Europe and Central Asia, Latin America, and the Middle East. His work has focused on housing finance strategies, subsidy reform, consumer protection, corporate governance, prudential oversight, and long-term funding frameworks. Earlier, he held senior positions at the Agency for Home Mortgage Lending in the Russian Federation and the GMAC Commercial Mortgage Corporation in the United States. He holds an MBA in finance and a BS in finance and computer science from Wilkes University in Pennsylvania.

ABOUT THE CONTRIBUTORS

Adalyat Abdumanapova is a corporate governance professional at the IFC, part of the World Bank Group, with more than 20 years of experience in advisory and consulting. She currently leads the IFC's Corporate Governance Advisory Program in Central Asia and Türkiye, overseeing strategic engagements with private sector companies, financial institutions, and quasi-state entities to strengthen governance frameworks and embed sustainability at the board and ownership levels. Adalyat advises on complex corporate governance transformations, board effectiveness, ownership and control structures, family governance and succession planning, state-owned enterprise governance, and sustainability-related governance reforms. Her work focuses on enhancing accountability, governance risk oversight, and long-term value creation in line with international best practices and IFC standards.
Adalyat holds an LLM from the University of Essex in the United Kingdom; a bachelor's degree in economics, management, and entrepreneurship from the International Academy of Business in Kazakhstan; and a bachelor's degree in business law from the Kazakh State Law Academy.

Akbobek Akhmedyarova is a researcher and quantitative modeler specializing in macroeconomic forecasting, dynamic stochastic general equilibrium (DSGE) modeling, econometric analysis, and policy simulation. As director of the Economic Modeling Center in the National Analytical Center at Nazarbayev University, she leads applied research for government decision-making, covering areas such as fiscal policy, regional strategy, and economic resilience. Her academic work spans behavioral economics, climate risk analytics, game-theoretic modeling, and DSGE models of Kazakhstan's housing market and energy transition.

Ganbaatar Jambal is a senior financial sector specialist with the Finance Competitiveness and Innovation Global Practice of the World Bank Group, Europe and Central Asia Unit. He specializes in banking supervision, risk management, economic modeling, and green finance. Ganbaatar joined the World Bank in 2015 and, since then, has worked on development projects implemented in the African, East Asia and Pacific, and Europe and Central Asia regions. Before joining the World Bank, Ganbaatar held various senior-level positions at the Central Bank of Mongolia, including director of the Regulation Policy Division, director General of Banking Supervision, chief economist, senior adviser to the Governor of the Central Bank, and chairman of the National Coordination Committee on Anti-Money Laundering. He has an MA in financial economics for public finance and a doctorate in economics.

Oleg Khe is a consultant in the Financial Institutions Group at the IFC, part of the World Bank Group. He has led financial planning, macroeconomic analysis, and forecasting in transformational and technical assistance IFC projects in Central Asia. Oleg has broad experience in strategy development for all types of financial institutions, as well as in strategy implementation and strategic projects' execution. His expertise is grounded in prolonged practical experience in financial planning, modeling, and analysis; International Financial Reporting Standards reporting; and financial control in top-tier banks and microfinance institutions (MFIs) in Russia. Oleg has participated in several key IFC projects in Central Asia, such as the transformation of leading MFIs in Kazakhstan into banks, long-term strategy development projects for insurance and corporate banking businesses of the top three players in Kazakhstan and Uzbekistan, and mortgage markets research and scenario forecasting in Kazakhstan and Uzbekistan. Before joining the IFC, Oleg managed the largest acquisition and transformation projects in the Russian banking sector. Korean by origin and a Russian national, he received a PhD in economics from the Peoples' Friendship University of Russia.

Chenyu Mao is an economist in the Fiscal Policy and Growth Global Practice at the World Bank. Her work focuses on the interaction between macroeconomic policies and financial systems and how they shape economic growth and financial stability in developing economies. In particular, she studies how policies affect credit allocation, monetary transmission, and debt dynamics across firms, banks, and sovereigns. Her research topics include zombie firms, subsidized mortgage programs, banking regulation, and sovereign debt vulnerabilities, drawing on detailed microlevel data. Her academic work has been published in peer-reviewed journals, including *Management Science.* Prior to joining the World Bank, she held positions at the International Monetary Fund, the Bank for International Settlements, and Goldman Sachs. A Chinese national, she holds a PhD in economics from the University of Maryland.

Victor Mints is a housing finance specialist in the Financial Institutions Group at the IFC, part of the World Bank Group, where he advises governments, central banks, and financial institutions in low-income countries on housing finance policy, housing products development, and infrastructure. Before joining IFC, Victor worked as a researcher, construction site manager, consultant, and banker. He has published in professional journals on topics related to housing finance and has spoken at international conferences. Victor holds a PhD in economics and management, an MBA in business administration, and an MSc in civil engineering.

Maria Turetskaya is a senior investment officer in the Financial Institutions Group of IFC, part of the World Bank Group. She focuses on financial sector development, including banking, capital markets, and small and medium enterprise finance across Central Asia and selected emerging markets. Maria has led and contributed to a range of investment and advisory engagements, including financial sector diagnostics, development of risk-sharing and guarantee instruments, and strategic transformation projects for financial institutions. Her work often involves structuring innovative financial solutions; supporting market development; and advising on strategy, business model optimization, operational efficiency, and access to finance. Prior to joining IFC, Maria worked in consulting, including the Boston Consulting Group and PwC, as well as in both public and private sector entities. Maria holds a degree in economics and is currently pursuing an executive master's degree in public administration at Sciences Po, with a focus on financial sector development and public policy.

Simon Walley is a lead financial sector specialist in the Finance, Competitiveness and Innovation Global Practice at the World Bank Group. While at the World Bank, he has led the Housing Finance Practice working with governments across Central Asia and Eastern Europe, the Middle East, and Sub-Saharan Africa. He has worked on affordable housing solutions by improving access to financial services, as well as has worked extensively on developing secondary mortgage markets through the creation of mortgage refinance companies, mortgage subsidy schemes, and housing microfinance. Prior to joining the World Bank, Simon worked in Brussels with the European Mortgage Federation as deputy secretary general, promoting the interests of mortgage lenders at the European level. He also worked as an economist for the Nationwide Building Society in the United Kingdom, which followed working as a banking regulator for the Bank of England and, later, the Financial Services Authority.

Executive Summary

Kazakhstan stands at a pivotal moment to modernize its housing finance system and unlock family investment in housing as part of its broader ambition to double the economy by 2029 and reach high-income status. Housing affordability remains a binding constraint despite sizable public support, reflecting structural inefficiencies in mortgage finance, subsidy design, and funding models. With a solid macrofinancial foundation and well-developed capital market infrastructure, Kazakhstan can rebalance its housing finance ecosystem—improving affordability outcomes while reducing fiscal costs and crowding in private capital.

MARKET CONTEXT AND KEY CHALLENGES

Kazakhstan's housing market faces strong demand, uneven supply, and affordability pressures. Real gross domestic product (GDP) growth has averaged about 5 percent in recent years, but high inflation and elevated interest rates have eroded household purchasing power. Mortgage lending is heavily concentrated in Almaty, Astana, and Shymkent—accounting for over half of new originations—while younger families and first-time homebuyers face high down-payment requirements and limited access to market-based mortgages.

Housing supply has grown steadily, averaging about 200,000 new units annually, yet affordability remains modest. Only about 20 percent of the richest households by income can afford a home using prevailing finance solutions, well below international benchmarks. Average housing prices in Almaty and Astana approach T 45 million (about US$88,000), far exceeding the borrowing capacity of most households without substantial resale equity. At the same time, fiscal space is tightening, with a significant budget deficit intensifying scrutiny of subsidy effectiveness.

MORTGAGE MARKET STRUCTURE AND THE ROLE OF OTBASY BANK

Kazakhstan's mortgage market totals over T 6 trillion (US$12 billion) and is split about evenly between Otbasy Bank's (OTB's) savings-and-loan (S&L) system and commercial second-tier banks. OTB dominates new origination with about 60 percent of mortgages, mainly funded by preferential deposits supported by public premiums. While this model has expanded access for targeted groups, it also crowds out commercial lending and limits market development.

The mortgage portfolio is young and untested through a full credit cycle, while capital-market-funding options—including covered bonds or mortgage-backed securities—are absent. As the OTB depositor base matures and fiscal backing is pressured, the current model faces constraints to scale sustainably without exposing the budget to rising long-term risks.

Governance arrangements further accentuate these risks. OTB's limited operational autonomy, shareholder intervention rights, and chief executive officer appointment structure diverge from Organisation for Economic Co-operation and Development (OECD) good practices for state-owned enterprises, weakening accountability and long-term strategic discipline.

PUBLIC SUBSIDIES: SCALE IS ADEQUATE, EFFICIENCY IS NOT

Public housing and housing finance subsidies are sizable—about T 950 billion (US$1.86 billion), or 0.7 percent of GDP—broadly in line with OECD norms. However, their design and targeting reduce impact. Subsidies often benefit higher-income households, are fragmented across programs, and frequently compete with rather than complement private finance. Programs such as the National Bank of Kazakhstan–funded 7-20-25 mortgage scheme have limited scale, weak targeting, and misalignment with monetary policy objectives.

The absence of a unified monitoring and evaluation framework means policy makers lack visibility on who benefits, at what fiscal cost, and with what affordability gains. As fiscal constraints tighten, improving the efficiency and targeting of public support is imperative.

A STRATEGIC REFORM AGENDA

The analysis points to a clear reform direction: Shift from a state-dominated, subsidy-heavy system toward a balanced housing finance ecosystem that leverages public resources to catalyze private capital and expand affordability.

Key priorities include

- *Strategic and governance reforms:* Establish a coordinated housing finance strategy, strengthen subsidy monitoring and evaluation, and align OTB governance with OECD and Basel standards to safeguard independence and risk management.
- *Rationalization and targeting of subsidies:* Better focus down-payment support on lower- and middle-income households, link S&L pricing to government bond rates for fiscal efficiency, restrict subsidies to once per household, and gradually phase out inefficient programs.
- *Market deepening and risk management:* Re-establish capital-market-funding channels (for example, covered bonds or securitization), introduce mortgage guarantees and insurance to de-risk lending, and expand products for borrowers with limited credit histories or informal incomes.

EXPECTED IMPACT

Taken together, these reforms could significantly improve housing affordability—potentially expanding access by 1–2 income deciles and benefiting 10–20 percent more households—while reducing long-term fiscal exposure. By reorienting subsidies toward de-risking and equity support rather than interest rate suppression, Kazakhstan can unlock private capital, strengthen financial stability, and enable more families to invest safely and sustainably in housing.

Overview and Key Messages

INTRODUCTION

Kazakhstan is at a strategic juncture to shape its residential mortgage market and advance key goals: housing affordability, fiscal efficiency, and greater private capital involvement. As Kazakhstan aims to double its economy by 2029 and reach high-income-country status, policy makers and market participants have a unique opportunity to modernize and deepen the mortgage ecosystem. They can accomplish this by mobilizing more private capital, refining the role of the savings and loan (S&L) system, building missing infrastructure, and making subsidies more targeted and efficient. The current structure of Kazakhstan's housing finance sector reflects an outsized role of public institutions and a suboptimal use of subsidies, which often distort the market and lack effective targeting.

Despite multiple public support programs, housing affordability remains a significant challenge. With a strong enabling environment and sector expertise, Kazakhstan is well positioned to change the market's prospects and expand access to affordable mortgage loans nationwide while at the same time pursuing greater fiscal efficiency and attracting more private capital into the mortgage market.

MACROECONOMIC AND HOUSING SUPPLY CONTEXT

Kazakhstan's housing market dynamics reflect the overall macroeconomic momentum, tightening fiscal space, and structural challenges in access to mortgages and affordability. Over the past three years, real gross domestic product (GDP) growth averaged 5 percent, yet high inflation eroded gains in household incomes, in turn undermining housing affordability. Access to residential housing is uneven, with about 55 percent of mortgages originating in Almaty, Astana, and Shymkent. High and volatile real estate prices, elevated interest rates, and limited housing supply restrict ownership opportunities, especially for young families and first-time homeowners, who typically lack a sufficient loan down payment. In the context of significant fiscal constraints (budget deficit of about US$7 billion, or 18 percent of revenues in 2024), policy makers and sector stakeholders are engaged in active public discussions regarding subsidy efficiency, allocation, and deployment mechanisms.

The homeownership rate is high at 97 percent, although housing adequacy of 23 m^2 per capita remains below regional comparators and significantly lags middle- and high-income countries. Kazakhstan's 6 million households reside primarily in single-family homes, and multi-apartment houses comprise 12 percent of the total housing stock of 2.5 million buildings. The recent annual average construction supply is approximately 200,000 units (apartments and individual homes), about 30 percent of which are financed by the state budget directly or through Kazakhstan Housing Company (KHC) for targeted mortgage financing by Otbasy Bank (OTB). The average price per square meter in Almaty and Astana reached almost T 600,000 (~US$1,200) in 2024,[1] while the country average without those two metropolitan statistical areas (MSAs) is just over T 350,000 (~US$684), or about 40 percent lower.[2] Given the average apartment size of 75 m^2, this brings average home prices in Almaty and Astana to about T 45 million (~US$88,000) and in other regions to about T 26 million (~US$50,000).

MORTGAGE MARKET STRUCTURE AND PRODUCTS

Kazakhstan's mortgage market comprises two segments roughly equal by portfolio size: mortgages from the OTB S&L system and mortgages from other, second-tier banks (STBs). In 2025, the aggregate portfolio outstanding—comprising about 400,000 loans—was over T 6 trillion (US$12 billion).[3] It has increased sevenfold over the past 10 years. Lending is concentrated geographically, with Almaty, Astana, and Shymkent accounting for over 50 percent of new loans. By lender, OTB accounts for about 60 percent of all mortgages issued in recent years. The mortgage portfolio is young (that is, "unseasoned"), as almost one-third of it (over T 2 trillion [US$3.9 billion], or about 130,000 loans) was originated in 2024—indicating that its current benign nonperforming loan (NPL) levels may significantly increase in the future.[4]

The dynamics of partial prepayments are unknown, but they can be presumed to be high. The lenders and market regulator estimate that, on average, loans are paid off in 5–8 years, while their average legal tenor is reportedly about 15 years. The average loan size of T 15–18 million (US$30,000–$35,000) is low relative to the average house price, which may indicate that most households cannot afford a new home without selling their old one to produce a large down payment; this, in turn, suggests that housing finance options for younger families or first-time homebuyers are limited.

Mortgage products vary in terms of interest rates, loan terms, and loan-to-value (LTV) ratios. OTB's S&L system offers targeted loans with interest rates as low as 2 percent, while conventional bank mortgages have rates of approximately 20 percent. The 7-20-25 program, financed by the National Bank of Kazakhstan (NBK), offers subsidized loans at 7 percent interest but accounts for only about 5 percent of recent yearly originations. Most mortgages have an annuity repayment schedule with a down-payment requirement ranging from 15 percent to 30 percent, although in practice, the common LTV ratio is in excess of 50 percent.[5] The reported average debt-to-income (DTI) ratio is 50 percent.[6]

All mortgages are in local currency. Notably, about 25 percent of mortgage originations are market priced, even in the face of high policy rates. Consequently, the market may exhibit upward dynamics if and when the cost of financial capital decreases. OTB funds its lending primarily from lower-cost deposits in its S&L system, while other STBs attract deposits on commercial terms.[7] This puts the STBs at a disadvantage, given higher deposit costs and the absence of a capital-market-funding option, as mortgage-backed instruments are nonexistent.

PUBLIC SUBSIDIES

Public housing sector subsidies—on both the demand and supply sides—are reasonable in volume but could benefit from optimization along several dimensions. As of 2024, the volume of housing and housing finance subsidies stood at about T 950 billion (US$2 billion);[8] this is just below 0.7 percent of the country's 2024 GDP and broadly in line with the Organisation for Economic Co-operation and Development (OECD) average of below 1 percent.[9]

However, subsidies' design, efficiency, and impact on affordability could benefit from certain adjustments, as detailed in the "Key Messages and Policy Options" section that follows. Among the key suggested modifications are (1) gradually phasing out the 7-20-25 program, (2) targeting budgetary down-payment subsidy (S&L deposit premium) only to lower- and middle-income depositors, (3) restructuring the S&L deposit and loan rate pricing to correlate with government bond rates (for newly originated loans only), and (4) increasing down-payment support by improving its targeting, without raising the aggregate subsidy volume for middle-income young families and first-time homebuyers outside the top-three MSAs (Almaty, Astana, and Shymkent).

HOUSING AFFORDABILITY

Housing affordability, a key metric of market effectiveness, is modest in Kazakhstan at 20 percent and restricts access to homeownership for lower- and middle-income families as well as first-time, young homebuyers.[10]

The market is shaped by state-owned institutions and subsidized programs that aim to increase affordability for households targeted by income and other socioeconomic factors. However, the public programs compete with, rather than complement, mortgage solutions offered by commercial banks.

Mortgages from banks—including joint programs with developers—as well as untargeted OTB S&L products can be utilized by the two richest population deciles (9th and 10th) based on income.[11] Mortgages under the NBK 7-20-25 program (for newly constructed properties only) can be obtained by borrowers in the top-six (from 6th to 10th) income deciles. Loans under subsidy programs administered by OTB are accessible to socially vulnerable and low-income population segments down to the 5th income decile.[12] With strong banking sector profitability (return on assets of 4.2 percent and return on equity of 28 percent) and low NPLs (3.6 percent), Kazakhstan's financial sector is well positioned to further enhance housing affordability and deepen the mortgage market.

OTBASY BANK'S ROLE AND BUSINESS MODEL

OTB, a national development finance institution, is a key provider of housing finance in Kazakhstan and the sole operator of state-supported mortgage programs. It was established in 2003 and became a subsidiary of the National Managing Holding "Baiterek" (Baiterek Holding) in 2013. OTB serves as a transmission mechanism for public subsidy programs, thus supporting socially vulnerable and low-income families. It operates a closed S&L system, encouraging long-term savings at low rates in exchange for preferential mortgage rates.[13] OTB benefits from budgetary support for its debt placements in the form of coupon cofinancing (over T 30 billion in 2025, or approximately US$59 million).[14] OTB mortgages have rates ranging from 2 percent to 14.4 percent, with loan terms of up to 25 years and a maximum loan amount of T 100 million (approximately US$200,000); some of these loans are affordable only for high-income families. By the end of 2024, OTB was the fourth-largest bank in Kazakhstan, with assets of T 4.28 trillion (US$8.4 billion), a mortgage portfolio exceeding T 3 trillion (US$6 billion), and over 3 million depositors.

Given the rapid growth in the OTB depositor base and its already high retail deposit market share, OTB may face limitations in continuing to grow its depositor base at the same pace.[15] This would leave shareholders and policy makers with two potential choices: either accept a decline or stagnation in mortgage originations—requiring a sharper focus on lower- and middle-income households as the main beneficiaries of public support—or enable OTB to expand lending through non-deposit funding sources such as debt issuance. The latter option carries significant risk because prevailing interest rate dynamics are incompatible with the S&L design and could potentially create long-term shareholder or budgetary exposure through bond coupon subsidies.

In October 2025, the media reported that the 2026 Kazakhstani state budget did not allocate funds for OTB deposit premiums, so the bank might need to use its own resources to pay these premiums for 2026 (InBusiness.kz 2025; Kursiv Media 2025). While the policy debate remains ongoing, the 2025 deposit premiums were fully paid from the budgetary sources (Otbasy Bank 2026). In February 2026, after this report was finalized, media further reported that OTB might start funding up to 50 percent of state deposit premiums from its own profits to reduce reliance on the state budget while also keeping premium rates unchanged (Kursiv Media 2026). While OTB currently has enough funds to cover the premiums, making this arrangement permanent could weaken the bank's financial position, limit its ability to issue new mortgages, and require a strategic overhaul. Given the absence of concrete information, the expected long-term impact is unclear. OTB and its shareholders might consider performing a thorough analysis of the situation, preferably together with a revision to the subsidy programs, including the depositor premium, as changes could affect depositor behavior and the effectiveness of housing policy.

OTBASY BANK'S CORPORATE GOVERNANCE CONSIDERATIONS

OTB operates under a governance structure designed to align its housing finance mandate with Kazakhstan's socioeconomic development goals, but this structure limits operational autonomy, exposes OTB to political interference, and compromises the independence and effectiveness of the Board of Directors (BoD) and Management Board. The chief executive officer (CEO) is appointed by the sole shareholder—contrary to the *OECD Guidelines on Corporate Governance of State-Owned Enterprises 2024* (OECD 2024), which recommend that boards hold authority over CEO appointments and dismissals. Without this mandate, the BoD cannot fully exercise oversight or assume responsibility for performance. Moreover, the bank's charter allows the sole shareholder to issue direct operational instructions and override BoD or management decisions, an arrangement that further conflicts with OECD principles for operational autonomy.

Strengthening OTB's corporate governance policies and practices in alignment with OECD guidelines and the Basel framework is critical. Key areas of focus include the role and composition of specialized board committees to ensure independence and robust risk management to safeguard the bank's autonomy from political influence and ensure its sustainable development. Effective corporate governance not only enhances the efficiency of the bank's financial and operational activities but also reinforces sound risk management, a strong internal control system, and comprehensive disclosure and transparency practices.

CAPITAL MARKET SOLUTIONS AND CREDIT RISK MANAGEMENT OPTIONS

The connection between mortgage and capital markets in Kazakhstan is currently weak, and there is good potential for reestablishing it. While OTB and KHC issue bonds, these are largely not market based and are not directly linked to housing finance assets. Kazakhstan's mortgage market currently lacks a functioning residential mortgage-backed securities (RMBS) market, despite the country's well-developed capital market infrastructure. Historically, Kazakhstan had active mortgage securitization, but after the global financial crisis, policy shifted toward an S&L model, which is not conducive to RMBS issuance. Covered bond legislation is absent, further restricting mortgage-financing options for banks.

Capital market solutions, such as covered bonds and RMBS, are common globally and offer alternative funding options for mortgage lenders. Reestablishing a robust capital-market-funding channel for mortgage finance could provide lenders with long-term liabilities, reduce credit and interest rate risk, and allow for portfolio growth beyond the banking system's capacity. While in Kazakhstan most mortgage originations are at below-market rates and not suited for capital market utilization, about 25 percent of originations are market priced and potentially eligible for securitization and covered bonds, which should be sufficient to jump-start the market.

Mortgage credit risk protection mechanisms, such as mortgage insurance (MI) and mortgage guarantees (MGs), are currently absent in Kazakhstan's market, even though they could help expand access for lower-income borrowers, those lacking a sufficient down payment, and people with informal incomes. Introducing these tools would allow more families to qualify for mortgages, efficiently transmit subsidies, and leverage public funds to attract significantly more private capital.

KEY MESSAGES AND POLICY OPTIONS

A comprehensive analysis of the Kazakhstani mortgage market's strengths, weaknesses, opportunities, and threats (SWOT) was conducted to evaluate policy options. The main objective underlying these options is the development of a more resilient and inclusive mortgage market that meets the needs of Kazakhstan's growing economy and diverse population—that is, a market that can increase housing affordability for households, decrease the fiscal burden, improve the effectiveness of public support programs, and boost private capital participation. The findings of the SWOT analysis are as follows:

- *Strengths* include a robust enabling environment for mortgage and capital markets, prudent lending practices, and a reasonable volume of public subsidies.

- *Weaknesses* include excessive state involvement and diluted subsidy focus, a persistent high-interest-rate environment, the high cost and short tenor of private financial capital, limited de-risking solutions, the absence of mortgage-backed capital market solutions, and mortgage loan portfolios with untested performance.
- *Opportunities* include an economic outlook that is generally positive (although tempered by fiscal constraints), market deepening through innovative product offerings (such as risk-sharing mechanisms), modernization of subsidy targeting and delivery, and continued digitalization of operations and customer access channels.
- *Threats* include macroeconomic volatility, fiscal shocks, and a potential decline in portfolio performance.

This report provides a high-level vision for further development of Kazakhstan's housing finance ecosystem, informed by the analysis of current practices, limitations, and alignment with international benchmarks and good practices. Housing affordability serves as the central metric throughout the analysis and underpins the proposed options for stakeholders' consideration. The suggested policy options aim to enhance housing affordability while rationalizing public support programs and mobilizing greater private capital. They focus on targeting subsidies toward housing solutions for lower- and middle-income families.

In parallel, these policy options aim to deepen the private mortgage market by reestablishing capital-market-funding channels, introducing risk-sharing mechanisms, and developing a regulatory framework for innovative products. These measures could be expected to increase the share of the population for whom housing is affordable by one to two income deciles—that is, to benefit 10–20 percent more households.

Policy options are presented in table O.1 and are described further below.

Strategic and governance reforms

Suggested policy options for strategic and governance reforms include the following:

1. Establish a clear and coordinated vision for developing the housing finance ecosystem through a sectoral strategy. When embodied in a sectoral strategy, this vision will serve as a foundation for alignment of stakeholders' efforts to ensure the efficient use of public support, engage private sector providers, and introduce a robust impact measurement framework. Designing and implementing a meaningful mortgage market development strategy (for example, as part of the Financial Sector Development Strategy or a national housing strategy) could be done jointly by the financial sector regulator and the government. The options listed below could become coordinated elements of such a strategy.

TABLE O.1 Policy options to accelerate mortgage market development, mobilize private capital, and enable family investment in housing

OPTION	RESPONSIBLE ENTITY
Strategic and governance reforms	
Establish a clear and coordinated vision for developing the housing finance ecosystem through a sectoral strategy	ARDFM, Baiterek, MIC, MNE, MoF, NBK
Introduce a robust M&E system for public support programs to ensure impact and fiscal efficiency	MIC, MNE, MoF
Conduct a full-scope review of OTB's corporate governance practices	Baiterek, MNE, OTB
Rationalization and targeting of public support	
Review the subsidy system, including its mechanics, targeting, transmission channels, and legal arrangements to improve efficiency of subsidies and strengthen their impact on affordability. For example, • Limit S&L premiums to lower- and middle-income households, and apply means testing. • Adjust S&L deposit and loan pricing to correlate with government bond rates for fiscal efficiency.	ARDFM, MIC, MNE, MoF
Introduce a targeted down-payment support program for lower- and middle-income clients across STBs	MIC, MoF
For all public support options and channels, restrict subsidies to one-time lifetime use per household and impose property transfer limitations	MIC, MNE, MoF
Gradually phase out the 7-20-25 program due to inefficiency and misalignment with NBK's mandate	NBK
Market deepening and innovation	
Reestablish a mortgage-backed capital-market-funding channel, potentially via a refinancing facility	ARDFM, Baiterek, KHC
Introduce mortgage credit risk guarantee and insurance mechanisms to support private lenders and underserved borrowers	ARDFM, Baiterek, KHC
Develop products for borrowers with informal incomes or limited credit histories, leveraging S&L strengths	OTB
Explore Islamic housing finance and related capital market solutions under appropriate regulatory frameworks	ARDFM, STBs
Conduct mortgage portfolio stress tests to manage systemic risk	ARDFM

Source: Original table for this publication.
Note: ARDFM = Agency of the Republic of Kazakhstan for Regulation and Development of Financial Market; Baiterek = Baiterek Holding; KHC = Kazakhstan Housing Company; M&E = monitoring and evaluation; MIC = Ministry of Industry and Construction; MNE = Ministry of National Economy; MoF = Ministry of Finance; NBK = National Bank of Kazakhstan; OTB = Otbasy Bank; S&L = savings and loan; STBs = second-tier banks.

2. Introduce a robust monitoring and evaluation (M&E) system for public support programs to ensure impact and fiscal efficiency; refer to Melecky et al. (2023) for details. Currently, M&E is rather fragmented and mostly oriented toward tracking preset quantitative indicators and intermediated volumes, without assessing socioeconomic impact and qualitative aspects. This likely incentivizes public institutions to expand their volume of business while competing with the private sector. M&E systems for public support programs (and the development finance institutions administering

them, such as KHC and OTB) should aim to measure additionality, fiscal efficiency in addressing market failures, and any increase in mortgage affordability. Sample metrics could include income profiles of subsidy recipients, spatial allocation of mortgages, the public-to-private capital cofinancing ratio, affordability of the deployed public support, and others.

3. Conduct a full-scope review and reform of OTB's corporate governance practices. A desktop review of OTB's corporate governance highlighted several areas at variance with good global practices. A full-scope analysis of the bank's corporate governance practices should be undertaken to ensure that findings and recommendations are complete and based on the effectiveness of actual practices.

Rationalization and targeting of public support

Suggested policy options for rationalization and targeting of public support include the following:

1. Conduct a comprehensive analysis of the housing finance subsidies—including their mechanics, targeting, and legal arrangements—to strengthen their impact on affordability. The issue of subsidies and their efficient use is especially relevant given the recent exclusion from the state budget of OTB (and, broadly, S&L) depositor premium contributions, as mentioned earlier. Because of the dearth of detailed information, at this point it is challenging to formulate OTB-specific areas of such reform, but it is likely that material adjustments to the mechanics and targeting of savings premium subsidies, along with the legal arrangements related to them, will need to be considered. In addition, OTB's management and shareholders will likely need to consider significant adjustments to the bank's business model and financial performance expectations. This analysis and potential adjustments to the S&L system should ideally be part of the comprehensive strategic approach to Kazakhstan's housing finance sector. Among issues to consider are the following:

   - *Limiting S&L premiums to lower- and middle-income households and applying means testing, together with product design and proxies such as loan amount or house price maxima.*[16] Currently, the down-payment subsidy benefits all members regardless of their income and chosen mortgage products, some of which allow for very high loan amount maxima and are affordable to only the top 10 percent of families by income.[17] Socially vulnerable households targeted under public programs, as well as first-time homebuyers, should continue to receive the premiums on their S&L savings. Once properly focused, premium levels may be adjusted upward to provide meaningful support to depositors on their path to homeownership.

   - *Adjusting S&L deposit and loan pricing to correlate with government bond rates for fiscal efficiency*. S&L deposit pricing and loan pricing are currently static at 2 percent and 5 percent, respectively. Periodically adjusting them to track government debt rate dynamics, as Germany does, could help protect the government budget and increase fiscal efficiency. Such a transition should not affect current OTB depositors; although the rates will change over time in line with monetary policy evolutions, they will also be fixed at contract-signing time, so the depositor should have clarity on both the deposit remuneration and the potential loan interest rate.

2. Introduce a targeted down-payment support program for lower- and middle-income clients across STBs.[18] This should help increase private sector market participation and subsidy efficiency. A down-payment subsidy (in the form of deposit premium) is currently exclusive to OTB S&L depositors. However, down-payment support need not be exclusive to the S&L system in general or to OTB in particular. Specifically, a down-payment subsidy could take the form of a copay from public resources that matches the borrower contribution of, for example, up to 15 percent of the property price. This effective doubling of the borrower's down payment reduces the loan amount and monthly payments and thus increases affordability. Such a mechanism also has a significant public-to-private capital multiplier, as the mortgage loan, as such, will be provided by the STBs.[19] In addition, mortgages at market rates with subsidized down payments (as compared to subsidized loans at below-market rates) are more liquid, that is, lenders can transfer or securitize them without discounting their price or requiring additional budget subsidies.

3. Restrict subsidies to one-time lifetime use, and impose property transfer limitations for all public support options and channels. Currently, borrowers can obtain a loan from the OTB S&L system more than once.[20] Given their savings and monthly repayment capacity, borrowers with higher incomes can benefit from down-payment support disproportionally more. Other forms of public housing finance support should also be extended only once per household. In addition, consideration should be given to restricting for a reasonable amount of time any transfer of a property obtained with subsidized mortgages.

4. Gradually phase out the 7-20-25 program, considering its inefficiency and misalignment with the NBK mandate. Following its recent downsizing, the program's yearly volume is T 100 billion (~US$195 million), or 5 percent of the recent yearly total originations; thus, the program is relatively small, as well as loosely targeted, fiscally inefficient, and apparently at odds with the stated NBK mandate.[21]

Market deepening and innovation

Suggested policy options for market deepening and innovation include the following:

1. Reestablish a mortgage-backed capital-market-funding channel, potentially via a refinancing facility. This may be a straightforward undertaking, given

that the relevant legal and regulatory framework is well developed, and stakeholders have experience. This step could be followed by securitization (by a refinancing facility or individual banks) and introduction of covered bonds. Harmonization of servicing and special-servicing practices may be beneficial to reduce credit and reputational risks and to maintain high levels of consumer protection. Although such a transition will likely benefit major private lenders (and not OTB, due to its low-yielding portfolio), overall impact on affordability and market development could be significant, given the potential influx of capital.

2. Introduce mortgage credit risk guarantee and insurance mechanisms to support private lenders and underserved borrowers. These market infrastructure elements facilitate market deepening primarily for private lenders, who are likely unfamiliar with borrowers in the middle- and lower-income segments of the market or with borrowers who have informal income. On the one hand, classical MI may provide down-payment support and may be a highly efficient subsidy mechanism for young families or others without a significant down payment. On the other hand, MGs may facilitate market deepening among borrowers with low and informal incomes. MGs are a highly efficient mechanism for subsidy transmission for lower-income or informal-income families and socially vulnerable borrowers.
3. Provide S&L mortgage products designed for borrowers with informal incomes or limited credit histories. The S&L system is, by its nature, supportive of borrowers with undocumented or informal incomes or without a credit history. It becomes even more supportive if coupled with a credit risk protection mechanism, such as an MG that can itself be an efficient subsidy transmission channel and that increases fiscal effectiveness and mobilizes private capital in tandem.
4. Explore Islamic housing finance and related capital market solutions under appropriate regulatory frameworks, such as with respect to consumer awareness and protection. A robust analysis of market demand and affordability impact should be undertaken before implementing any of these solutions.
5. Conduct mortgage portfolio stress tests to manage systemic risk. Given the uncertain near-term macroeconomic dynamics, such stress tests could be used to assess potential capital consumption and social impact under likely and worst-case scenarios. Developer-linked mortgage loans could pose elevated levels of risk and require attention from the banking supervisor. Notably, mortgage portfolio analytical methods and conventions should be standardized across the industry, and key results and data should be periodically published—especially given the development of capital-market-funding activities—for the benefit of the investor and analyst community.

NOTES

1. Here and throughout, the average exchange rate as of the first half of 2025 is US$1 = T 512 (National Bank of Kazakhstan 2025).
2. According to KHC.
3. KHC data as of January 2025.
4. Mortgage default levels usually increase up to the peak (worst default levels) at 40–60 months of the portfolio life cycle. This is a universal pattern for mortgage loan performance observed in virtually all markets. It is likely that mortgage portfolios in Kazakhstan exhibit similar behavior.
5. The *LTV ratio,* a key mortgage loan characteristic, is the ratio of the loan amount to the independently assessed market value of the collateral property. Typical prudent values globally are 70–80 percent; higher values are considered risky and often require additional credit risk protection mechanisms, such as mortgage insurance or guarantee.
6. The *DTI ratio,* another key mortgage loan characteristic, is the ratio of mandatory periodic (typically monthly) loan repayment and other amounts relative to borrower household income, often net of non-mortgage mandatory expenses. The prudent ratio globally is around 30–50 percent, although values vary significantly by country.
7. OTB deposits are provided at lower interest rates than those available on the open market. As of October 2025, total OTB liabilities were reported at over T 4 trillion; several outstanding OTB bond issuances account for T 160 billion, or less than 5 percent, of this amount.
8. The T 950 billion figure is based on Prime Minister of the Republic of Kazakhstan (2024) and Trend News Agency (2024). The conversion of tenge to US dollars uses the average 2024 exchange rate of 470:1; refer to Exchange-Rates.org (2024).
9. The OECD average is about 1 percent relative to GDP. Refer to the OECD Affordable Housing Database at https://www.oecd.org/en/data/datasets/oecd-affordable-housing-database.html and the OECD Social Expenditure Database at https://www.oecd.org/en/data/datasets/social-expenditure-database-socx.html. Precise numbers are challenging to ascertain because not all public support is reported and some duplications occur. Individual country numbers vary significantly.
10. The 20 percent figure takes into account unsubsidized finance solutions. Of the many definitions of housing affordability that exist, one of the more robust and policy-focused ones is used in this report. Affordability is measured as a percentage of the population by income that can afford to obtain a suitable dwelling using prevailing housing finance solutions. In a balanced—that is, effective—market situation, a median (50 percent) of the population by income can prudently obtain a home of median price. Practicality and lack of proper data often necessitate using average house prices instead of actual house prices at which mortgages are originated. Thus, affordability at 20 percent in Kazakhstan—compared to what should be a policy target of 50 percent—is quite modest.
11. OTB's untargeted products are available to all OTB depositors and lack the eligibility criteria of OTB's targeted public subsidy programs.
12. Families in deciles 1–4 are generally considered "low income," those in deciles 5–8 are considered "middle income," and those in deciles 9–10 are considered "high income."
13. According to OTB, its depositors receive an annual deposit premium directly from the Ministry of Finance—a down-payment subsidy—of up to T 157,000 (US$307), or 200 times the monthly calculation amount. In 2025, this amounted to T 124.4 billion (US$243 million), with a 5-year average of T 72 billion (US$141 million).

14. Coupon cofinancing is laid out in Order 190 (refer to Minister of Industry and Construction of the Republic of Kazakhstan 2024). The T 30 billion figure is based on staff calculations using OTB data.
15. According to OTB, 3.4 million Kazakhstanis, or approximately one-third of the economically active population, currently have deposits with Otbasy Bank.
16. For example, the property price maximum as appraised by a licensed independent valuer could be set at the national average selling price for the previous year (or a practical shorter time period). This would incentivize more transactions outside the major metropolitan statistical areas and likely reduce the motivation of families in the top income deciles to use S&L facilities.
17. Loan amounts reach up to T 100 million, while the average OTB loan amount is T 15 million.
18. A public down-payment copay effectively increases borrower equity and reduces the loan amount, so that, even in the context of high interest rates, periodic mortgage payments can be reduced to match household incomes. This approach increases affordability without sacrificing mortgage loan liquidity (as the interest rate is market priced), and it makes the loan suitable for capital market utilization.
19. This effect depends on the exact mechanics—for example, budgetary down-payment support that matches borrower savings would have affordability impact equal to or better than a nominally low interest rate.
20. The NBK 7-20-25 program, on the other hand, explicitly limits program eligibility to once per lifetime.
21. The program carries an annual mortgage interest rate of 7 percent, compared with banks' interest rates of about 20 percent.

REFERENCES

Exchange-Rates.org. 2024. "US Dollar (USD) to Kazakhstan Tenge (KZT) Exchange Rate History for 2024." https://www.exchange-rates.org/exchange-rate-history/usd-kzt-2024.

InBusiness.kz. 2025. "Деньги на премии клиентам Отбасы банка не предусмотрели в госбюджете." October 22, 2025. https://inbusiness.kz/ru/last/dengi-na-premii-klientam-otbasy-banka-ne-predusmotreli-v-gosbyudzhete.

Kursiv Media. 2025. "Госпремию по вкладам в Отбасы банке не будут выплачивать из бюджета." October 22, 2025. https://kz.kursiv.media/2025-10-22/svan-kto-budet-platit-gospremiyu-po-vkladam-v-otbasy-banke-rasskazali-v-minfine.

Kursiv Media. 2026. "Госпремии в Отбасы банке хотят выплачивать по-новому." February 17, 2026. https://kz.kursiv.media/2026-02-17/zhnb-v-kazahstane-mogut-izmenit-shemu-vyplat-gospremii-po-vkladam-v-otbasy-banke/.

Melecky, Martin, Pasquale Di Benedetta, Ismael Ahmad Fontan, Ganbaatar Jambal, and Michel Noel. 2023. *Braced for Impact: Reforming Kazakhstan's National Financial Holding for Development Effectiveness and Market Creation*. World Bank Group. https://openknowledge.worldbank.org/entities/publication/afbb7e36-ad92-4205-9b91-715eb4bd00e8.

Minister of Industry and Construction of the Republic of Kazakhstan. 2024. "On Approval of the Rules for subsidizing the coupon interest rate on bonds issued by the issuer for further issuance of housing mortgage loans for the purpose of improving housing conditions in accordance with the legislation of the Republic of Kazakhstan," Order of the Minister of Industry and Construction of the Republic of Kazakhstan, May 24, 2024, No. 190. https://adilet.zan.kz/rus/docs/V2400034409.

National Bank of Kazakhstan. 2025. "Official Foreign Exchange Rates on Average for the Period." https://nationalbank.kz/en/news/oficialnye-kursy.

OECD (Organisation for Economic Co-operation and Development). 2024. *OECD Guidelines on Corporate Governance of State-Owned Enterprises 2024*. OECD Publishing. https://doi.org/10.1787/18a24f43-en.

Otbasy Bank. 2026. "591 709 вкладчиков Отбасы банка получили максимальную премию государства." March 3, 2026. https://hcsbk.kz/ru/news/publications/591-709-vkladchikov-otbasy-banka-poluchili-maksimalnuyu-premiyu-gosudarstva/.

Prime Minister of the Republic of Kazakhstan. 2024. "Support for Housing Construction at Expense of Kazakhstan Housing Company JSC Totalled 640.3 Billion Tenge." December 10, 2024. https://primeminister.kz/en/news/support-for-housing-construction-at-expense-of-kazakhstan-housing-company-jsc-totalled-6403-billion-tenge-29450.

Trend News Agency. 2024. "Kazakhstan Reveals Allocations for Housing Construction in 2024." April 23, 2024. https://www.trend.az/casia/kazakhstan/3889769.html.

Abbreviations

ALM	asset liability management
ARDFM	Agency of the Republic of Kazakhstan for Regulation and Development of Financial Market
Baiterek	Baiterek Holding
BoD	Board of Directors
CEO	chief executive officer
CIS	Commonwealth of Independent States
CRM	credit risk mitigation
CRO	chief risk officer
DSGE	dynamic stochastic general equilibrium
DTI	debt-to-income
ESG	environmental, social, governance
FGTS	Fundo de Garantia do Tempo de Serviço (Severance Indemnity Fund)
GDP	gross domestic product
HPA	house price appreciation
IFC	International Finance Corporation
KHC	Kazakhstan Housing Company
KIK	Kazakhstan Mortgage Company
KLGF	Kazakhstan Mortgage Loan Guarantee Fund
LTV	loan-to-value
M&E	monitoring and evaluation
MB	Management Board
MCA	monthly calculation amount
MFI	microfinance institution
MG	mortgage guarantee
MI	mortgage insurance
MIC	Ministry of Industry and Construction

MNE	Ministry of National Economy
MoF	Ministry of Finance
MSA	metropolitan statistical area
n.a.	not applicable
NAR	National Association of Realtors
NBK	National Bank of Kazakhstan
NMH	National Managing Holding
NPL	nonperforming loan
OECD	Organisation for Economic Co-operation and Development
OTB	Otbasy Bank
P&I	principal and interest
PITI	principal, interest, taxes, insurance
PTI	payment-to-income
PV	present value
RMBS	residential mortgage-backed securities
S&L	savings and loan
SBPE	Brazilian Savings and Loan System
SFH	Sistema Financeiro da Habitação (Housing Finance System)
SFI	Sistema de Financiamento Imobiliário (Real Estate Financing System)
SOE	state-owned enterprise
STB	second-tier bank
SWOT	strengths, weaknesses, opportunities, threats
T	Kazakhstani tenge
UK	United Kingdom
US	United States

Average exchange rate as of the first half of 2025: US$1 = T 512.

1 Kazakhstan's Economic and Housing Market Context

MACROECONOMIC CONTEXT

Kazakhstan's ambitious goal to double its economy by 2029 is supported by solid GDP growth of 4–5 percent annually, yet persistently high inflation (averaging 11–12 percent), a restrictive monetary policy stance with rates at 18 percent, and dominant state-owned enterprises continue to undermine private sector competitiveness and household purchasing power. Fiscal and current account deficits are projected to shrink temporarily in 2026 and then revert to long-term elevated averages, keeping financial conditions tight and long-term borrowing costs elevated. These dynamics are feeding directly into the housing market, where high mortgage rates, rising construction costs, and subdued demand are expected to further erode housing affordability.

Key conditions and challenges

Kazakhstan has adopted a bold strategy to accelerate growth and aims to double its economy by 2029 compared to 2023 levels. Nonetheless, excessive state interventions in the market and the dominant positions of state-owned enterprises continue to distort competition and adversely affect private sector investments and productivity. Therefore, it is crucial to restrict state interventions to traditional key roles: addressing market and coordination failures and delivering public goods—for example, by investing in human capital, facilitating innovation and the adoption of new technologies, and constructing essential infrastructure.

This approach can enhance firms' productivity and contribute to their climate mitigation and adaptation efforts, thereby improving their competitiveness. Consequently, the recent high-level decision to liberalize the economy marks a step in the right direction. These liberalization efforts also concern the residential mortgage loan market (the focus of this report), which enables households to invest in property, accumulate assets, and improve their living conditions.

Outlook

Kazakhstan's post-COVID-19 recovery has been underpinned by expansion of oil production and fiscal stimulus; these have delivered robust real gross domestic product (GDP) growth of about 4–5 percent annually. Over the medium term, growth is expected to converge toward its potential at a still-solid 3–4 percent rate. However, recent data suggest that strong headline growth has not translated into higher real household incomes or improved housing affordability. This disconnect primarily reflects persistently high inflation—averaging around 11–12 percent, well above the 5 percent medium-term target.

In response, the National Bank of Kazakhstan (NBK) has maintained a restrictive monetary stance, lifting the policy rate to 18 percent in October 2025 and signaling a willingness to keep conditions tight until disinflation is firmly established. Therefore, in the near term, elevated inflation is likely to further erode real incomes, constraining housing affordability.

The fiscal deficit is set to shrink too to 1.3 percent of GDP, before increasing to 2.8 percent in 2027–28. This trend, driven by still-weak non-oil revenues and higher quasi-fiscal outlays, partly offsets the monetary tightening. Externally, the current account deficit is expected to narrow to 0.4 percent of GDP in 2026 amid higher prices of major export commodities, including oil. Rising net investment income outflows could increase pressures related to the balance of payments, increasing the likelihood of further drawdowns from the National Fund. These factors point to persistently tight financial conditions and elevated risk premia, which limit the scope for a swift decline in long-term borrowing costs.

As a result, spillovers to the housing market are likely to be adverse, particularly outside major urban centers. Elevated policy rates and strong pass-through to banks' funding costs are likely to keep mortgage rates high, dampening mortgage credit growth. At the same time, elevated construction costs weigh on housing affordability, and developers are likely to remain cautious amid shallow demand. Absent targeted measures to alleviate supply constraints and enhance access to finance, the current macroeconomic dynamics and future trends are unlikely to lead to gains in housing affordability or a durable strengthening of the housing market (refer to the analysis in box 1.1).

Implications of housing market dynamics for Kazakhstan's economy

The analysis using the macroeconomic model described in box 1.1 underscores that Kazakhstan's economic growth remains closely linked to developments in the oil sector. However, government support programs combined with housing market dynamics are starting to have significant implications for macroeconomic stability. The interplay between oil prices, mortgage subsidy policies, and household consumption patterns is central to the transmission of economic shocks.

Box 1.1

Housing market analysis using a dynamic stochastic general equilibrium model

A dynamic stochastic general equilibrium (DSGE) model for Kazakhstan was used to investigate the interplay among economic growth, inflation, and housing market dynamics. The model is calibrated to Kazakhstan's economic conditions; by integrating the oil sector and government subsidies, it explains the transmission mechanisms of both global and domestic shocks and identifies critical policy levers.

Key results include the following:

- *Model performance.* The model demonstrates a robust historical fit, effectively replicating key macroeconomic episodes, including the 2015–16 oil price downturn, the 2020 recession induced by the COVID-19 pandemic, and the 2022 inflation surge.
- *Sectoral implications.* Dynamics of the DSGE model have notable implications for the housing and construction sectors, which collectively account for approximately 14 percent of gross domestic product (GDP). Model estimates suggest that these sectors contribute around 0.13 percent to overall GDP growth, indicating significant potential for productivity improvements that could further accelerate economic expansion.
- *Inflation dynamics.* The analysis shows that inflation is sensitive to changes in subsidized mortgage rates, with an estimated elasticity of 0.32. While mortgage subsidies provide important social benefits, they can also lead to macroeconomic risks by increasing inflationary pressures. Indeed, the analysis provides evidence that housing market factors have contributed to recent inflationary pressures.

Regarding sources of volatility, model estimates indicate that oil price fluctuations account for approximately 80 percent of observed GDP volatility, underscoring the economy's significant exposure to external commodity price shocks. It is worth noting that, under certain scenarios, roughly 10 percentage points of the remaining volatility are driven by housing subsidy policies and changes in household preferences. This finding indicates that further robustness checks and sensitivity testing are warranted.

Periods of rising oil prices tend to boost household incomes and fiscal revenues, yet they also contribute to inflationary pressures through heightened housing demand and credit expansion. Conversely, productivity gains support sustainable economic growth without intensifying inflation, indicating that long-term resilience requires diversification beyond the oil sector.

The housing sector plays a dual role in the economy: it drives growth and employment, but also amplifies volatility when policy or credit conditions change. Notably, housing price dynamics are predominantly influenced by domestic factors that could be subject to policy optimizations, whereas global oil markets are inherently unpredictable.

Three main lessons can be distilled from the macro modeling exercise:

1. *Productivity drives long-run growth dynamics.* The model shows that economies like Kazakhstan's, reliant on commodity revenues, are exposed to

volatility, and also that productivity improvements—through innovation, technology adoption, and more efficient labor allocation—generally yield more stable, diversified growth trajectories. Higher productivity consistently raises potential output and reduces sensitivity to external shocks.

2. *Housing policies have meaningful stabilization effects but carry macrofinancial risks.* Simulations show that mortgage subsidies and other housing-support mechanisms can boost short-term demand and improve household welfare. However, when applied during periods of strong credit growth or supply constraints, these measures can amplify inflationary pressures and elevate vulnerabilities in construction lending and household balance sheets. The housing market thus acts as both a stabilizer and a channel for overheating.
3. *Inflation-focused monetary policy anchors macroeconomic stability, but interactions with housing interventions matter.* The modeling confirms that maintaining a clear anti-inflation bias helps stabilize expectations and reduce output volatility. At the same time, scenarios in which the central bank is directly involved in housing market support entail greater policy trade-offs, with weaker transmission of interest rate adjustments and more persistent inflation. Better alignment across monetary, fiscal, and housing-related instruments yields more balanced, predictable macro outcomes.

BANKING SECTOR DEVELOPMENTS

Kazakhstan's financial system has undergone notable changes in recent years. The establishment of the Agency of the Republic of Kazakhstan for Regulation and Development of the Financial Market (ARDFM) in 2020 strengthened oversight by improving supervisory practices and enhancing transparency through the regular publication of asset quality reviews, Supervisory Review and Evaluation Process reports, and stress test results. At the same time, the digitalization of payments and financial services accelerated—driven by NBK initiatives to improve efficiency and expand access, as well as by behavioral shifts during the COVID-19 period. However, post-pandemic recovery measures and the rapid expansion of digital finance have also been accompanied by a marked increase in state involvement in the financial sector, raising concerns about market distortions and weakened competition.

By end-2025, Kazakhstan's banking sector comprised 23 banks, including 15 with foreign participation and only one fully state owned. Total bank assets have been expanding at 15–20 percent annually, with loans reaching T 40.2 trillion (US$8 billion), or 57 percent of banking assets. Lending to individuals accounted for 44 percent of total loans (T 24.8 trillion or US$5 billion), while mortgages represented 17 percent (T 7 trillion, or US$13 billion). Despite rapid portfolio growth—supported by rising deposits and state programs—overall credit stood at about 27 percent of GDP, still low relative to peers. Asset quality remained solid, with nonperforming loans at 3.6 percent and provisions covering 60 percent. Bank profitability was strong, with return on assets at 4.2 percent and return on equity at 28 percent, underpinned by high margins in consumer lending. Ongoing digitalization continued to lower delivery costs and expand access. The sector also maintained sizable buffers: In 2025, the capital adequacy ratio was 20 percent (well above the 12 percent requirement), and high-quality liquid assets accounted for roughly 30 percent of total assets.[1] Bank competition in Kazakhstan's mortgage market has intensified as more lenders have expanded into retail housing finance, and rapid digitalization has further sharpened this competition by lowering service costs, streamlining mortgage approval processes, and allowing borrowers to compare and access loan offerings more easily.

HOUSING SUPPLY AND DEMAND

Although homeownership in Kazakhstan is exceptionally high at 97 percent, average living space remains limited at 23 m^2 per person, well below regional and global norms. Of the country's 6 million households, most live in single-family homes, and multi-apartment buildings make up only 12 percent of the 2.5 million housing structures. This situation contributes to both the high ownership rate and the ongoing adequacy gap in per capita living space.

The state plays an important role in supporting housing construction. The recent annual average construction supply was close to 200,000 units (apartments and individual homes). About 30 percent of these units are financed directly from the state budget and through the Kazakhstan Housing Company (KHC) for subsequent socially targeted mortgage financing by Otbasy Bank (OTB).

In 2024, just under 19 million m^2 of living space (over 250,000 units) entered the market.[2] The Ministry of Construction financed about 10 percent of that volume, and about 40,000 apartments (roughly 20 percent of the total) were supported by the KHC.

As illustrated in box 1.2, KHC has a number of support options for developers and borrowers. One particular business line—construction completion guarantees—is rather small in scale and covers only about 7,000 units (apartment or homes). Moreover, recent legislative changes to allow use of an escrow account scheme for off-plan (unfinished construction) house purchases may end any demand for such guarantees.

Regional disparities in residential property prices across Kazakhstan reflect the concentration of economic activity and housing demand in major urban centers. In 2024, the average price per square meter in Almaty and Astana—the two largest cities by population—reached about T 600,000 (~US$1,200), while the country average without those two metropolitan statistical areas was just over T 350,000, or about 40 percent lower.[3] Given an average apartment size of 75 m^2, average home prices in Almaty and Astana are about T 45 million (~US$88,000), while in other regions they are about T 26 million (~US$50,000). Thus, given an average mortgage amount of about T 15–18 million (~US$65,000), a large share of loans appears to have originated with a down payment of over 50 percent, possibly obtained by the borrowers from the sale of a previous dwelling.[4]

Box 1.2

Activities of the Kazakhstan Housing Company

The Kazakhstan Housing Company, a state-owned enterprise owned by Baiterek Holding, supports the growth of affordable housing supply and has a meaningful impact on the market, particularly its affordable segment. Its 2024 activities included the following:

- Issuance of construction completion guarantees (32 policies covering about 7,000 units, or 3 percent of all new units)
- Provision of subsidies to private developers (about 1,000 units, or 0.5 percent of total new units)
- Financing of affordable housing construction, primarily for a rent-to-own scheme via Otbasy Bank (26,000 units, or 13 percent of total new units)
- Provision of support for modernizing existing housing (about 6,000 units)

Source: Kazakhstan Housing Company (2024).

On the one hand, this situation illustrates low affordability per se, since the mortgages available to borrowers cover less than half the cost of an average house or apartment. In other words, existing housing finance solutions—in the context of high interest rates—require borrowers to make a large down payment to lower the loan amount and make monthly payments affordable. In this environment, young families or first-time homebuyers face a significant challenge in obtaining a mortgage, as they are likely to lack savings.

On the other hand, the high average down payment (implied in the significant difference between average apartment price and average mortgage loan amount) shows that Kazakhstani families adapt and manage to use mortgage products even when interest rates are high. They do so by accumulating funds for a large down payment, either by saving at OTB for an extended period or by selling an existing house and "upsizing"—that is, obtaining a loan for a larger home while selling the existing smaller one, which is common practice globally.

HOUSING PRICE DYNAMICS

Core inflation–adjusted house price appreciation (HPA) for new construction has been volatile and negative over the last 15 years.[5] As illustrated in figure 1.1, real housing prices in the Astana and Almaty regions, as well as in Kazakhstan overall, have been quite volatile, owing in part to sudden and significant spikes in demand. In 2021, for example, it became possible to withdraw pension savings for housing finance purposes, a reform that significantly expanded households' ability to accumulate down payments and spurred greater participation in the formal mortgage market (E.gov 2025).

FIGURE 1.1

Real house price dynamics in Kazakhstan, 2011–24 (new construction)

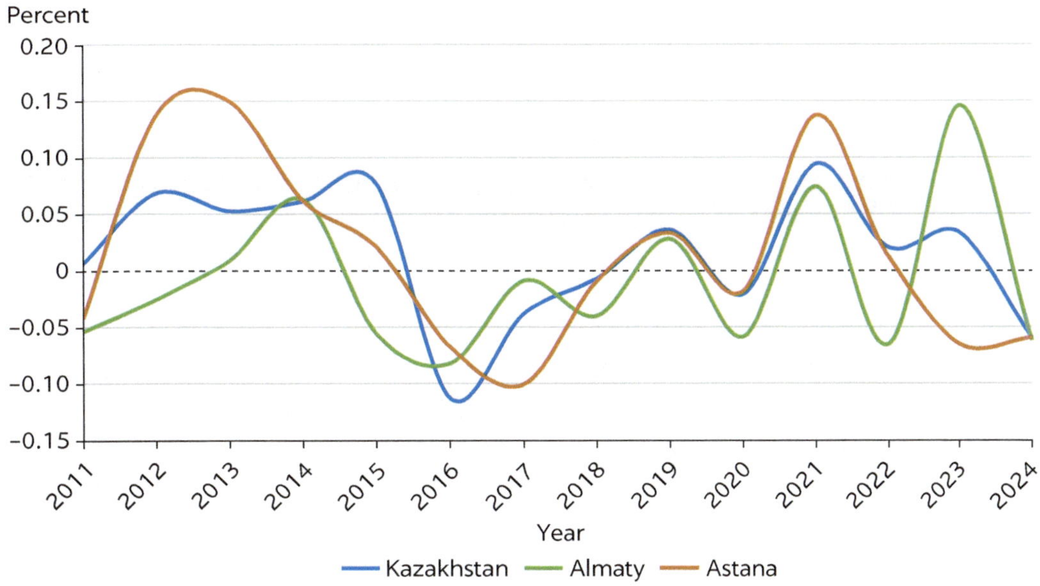

Sources: Original figure for this publication using data from the Agency for Strategic Planning and Reforms of the Republic of Kazakhstan; the Bureau of National Statistics; the National Bank of Kazakhstan; and World Bank Group calculations.

This market risk dynamic is relevant to property buyers and developers, as well as to KHC, a significant provider of public support for the residential real estate market. Investors in residential real estate may find themselves in a situation where the asset class does not provide inflation protection. In such an environment, households may shift their focus from viewing housing as an investment hedge to prioritizing the long-term security and stability of homeownership, which can, in turn, support a more sustainable housing finance market—particularly if homeownership itself remains the primary objective rather than short-term capital gains.

Developers, on the other hand, face significant market risk, which may motivate them to accelerate off-plan (unfinished property) sales, a practice that likely elevates completion risks for buyers. The adoption of an escrow account scheme for such sales—where buyers' funds are transferred to the developer upon completion of construction—is a welcome development. In this regard, authorities and KHC shareholders may wish to consider adopting a countercyclical approach, especially given policy measures that may lead to a significant and rapid inflow of housing finance. Such an approach may prove challenging, however, as it requires robust coordination with other stakeholders, preferably in the context of a sectoral development strategy.

The nominal HPA for existing-home dynamics is relevant to mortgage lenders, borrowers, and the market regulator. As illustrated in figure 1.2, home prices are volatile and show a significant amplitude of about 30 percent in short periods.

This market risk dynamic is relevant for portfolio analytics and supervision, including collateral adequacy and capital consumption, as well as for the pricing of mortgage credit risk protection. Mortgage prepayment speed seems high because loans with an average legal tenor of just under 15 years reportedly fully amortize in about 8 years.[6] But lenders may face a significant decline in property prices, materially elevating portfolio loan-to-value (LTV) levels.

This risk is particularly relevant for certain portfolio vintages (year of origination). After 2021, nominal property prices declined by about 20 percent on average, and, thus, originally prudent LTV ratios likely deteriorated significantly. In this regard, financial sector authorities might consider verifying relevant bank-level and systemwide assumptions about mortgage portfolio stress test scenarios.

FIGURE 1.2

Nominal house price movements in Kazakhstan, 2011–24 (secondary sales)

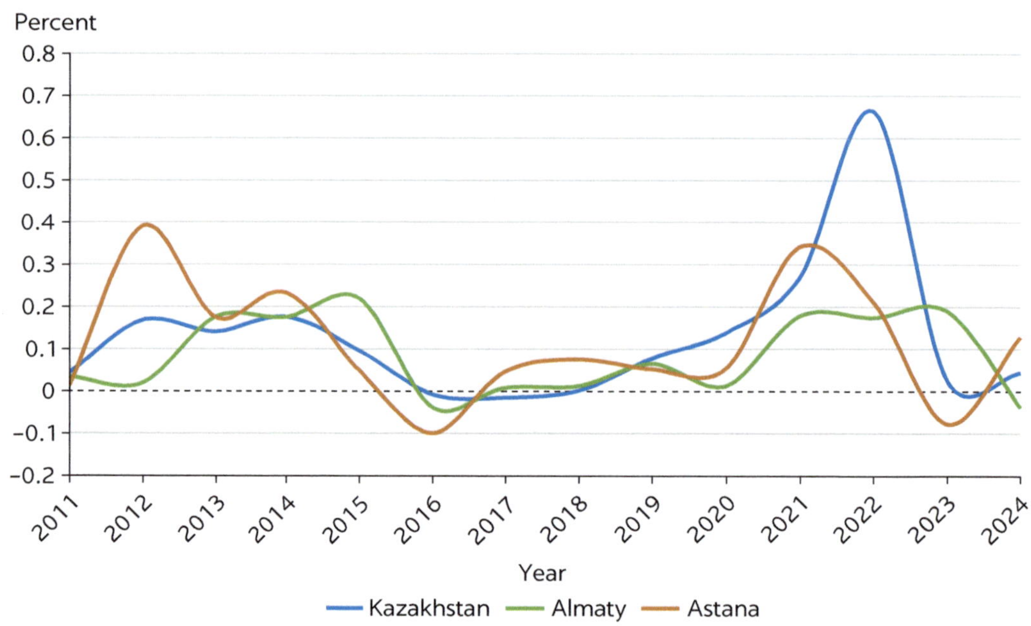

Sources: Original figure for this publication using data from the Agency for Strategic Planning and Reforms of the Republic of Kazakhstan; the Bureau of National Statistics; the National Bank of Kazakhstan; and World Bank Group calculations.

NOTES

1. Based on information from ARDFM.
2. Based on information from KHC.
3. Based on information from KHC.
4. The average house or apartment should cost about T 45 million, and with a reasonable loan-to-value ratio of 75 percent, an average mortgage loan should be about T 35 million. In reality, an average loan is about half of that, as reported by OTB and other second-tier banks. Data are likely skewed by OTB products (one-half of originations) with a required 50 percent down payment.
5. NBK's methodology for estimating the core consumer price index is described in Orlov and Seydakhmetov (2023).
6. Based on information from ARDFM.

REFERENCES

E.gov. 2025. "The Targeted Use of Pension Savings for Improving Housing Conditions. Covering Medical Expenses. And Transferring Pension Assets to Trust Management." August 13, 2025. https://egov.kz/cms/en/articles/pension_saving.

Kazakhstan Housing Company. 2024. *Annual Report 2024*. https://khc.kz/upload/iblock/13f/4ivsm738otlvnrj55qrtmojaw6gknde7.pdf.

Orlov, K., and A. Seydakhmetov. 2023. "Various Estimates of Core Inflation for Kazakhstan" [in Russian]. National Bank of Kazakhstan Working Paper 2023-02. February 8, 2023. https://nationalbank.kz/ru/news/issledovaniya?page=4.

2 Kazakhstan's Housing Finance Market Evolutions

MARKET OVERVIEW

Kazakhstan's residential mortgage market has been evolving along two distinct paths. The sector is composed of two roughly equal segments by loan originations and portfolio outstanding: (1) mortgages under the savings and loan (S&L) system operated by Otbasy Bank (OTB) and (2) mortgages from other second-tier banks (STBs). The latter includes loans under a significantly subsidized program financed by the National Bank of Kazakhstan (NBK), classic market-priced mortgages, and loans for purchase of apartments under construction with a lower-than-market interest rate.

The residential mortgage loan portfolio has seen significant growth over the past 10 years. While the overall portfolio has grown almost sevenfold, OTB's market share has gradually increased as well, as shown in figure 2.1. This increase may have been driven both by exogenous factors, such as increased market interest rates, and endogenous factors, such as an overall increase in OTB membership over time with commensurate growth in lending.[1]

Kazakhstan's housing finance portfolio is concentrated both geographically and by lender. In recent years, over half (54 percent) of loans by monetary value were issued for properties in Almaty and Astana, while about 60 percent of all loans were originated by OTB. Key lenders include OTB and eight private banks; over the past 5 years, the former has consistently held more than 50 percent of market share by portfolio outstanding. Total 2024 originations amounted to T 2,023 billion (~US$4 billion), or about 130,000 loans, given the estimated average loan amount of T 15 million (~US$30,000).[2] OTB extended about 80,000 loans, or 60 percent of the market's total. The market share of the top-three banks (excluding OTB) is about 30 percent. Mortgages are in local currency and predominantly have an annuity ("level pay") repayment schedule. The average loan tenor is 180 months (15 years), with an interest rate of about 20 percent a year. Portfolio performance in the aggregate remains robust; the reported share of nonperforming loans (NPLs) is below 1 percent. However, given the portfolio's low seasoning (it is a young portfolio), these data may not be indicative of future performance.

FIGURE 2.1

Composition of the outstanding mortgage portfolio, 2015–24 (T, billions)

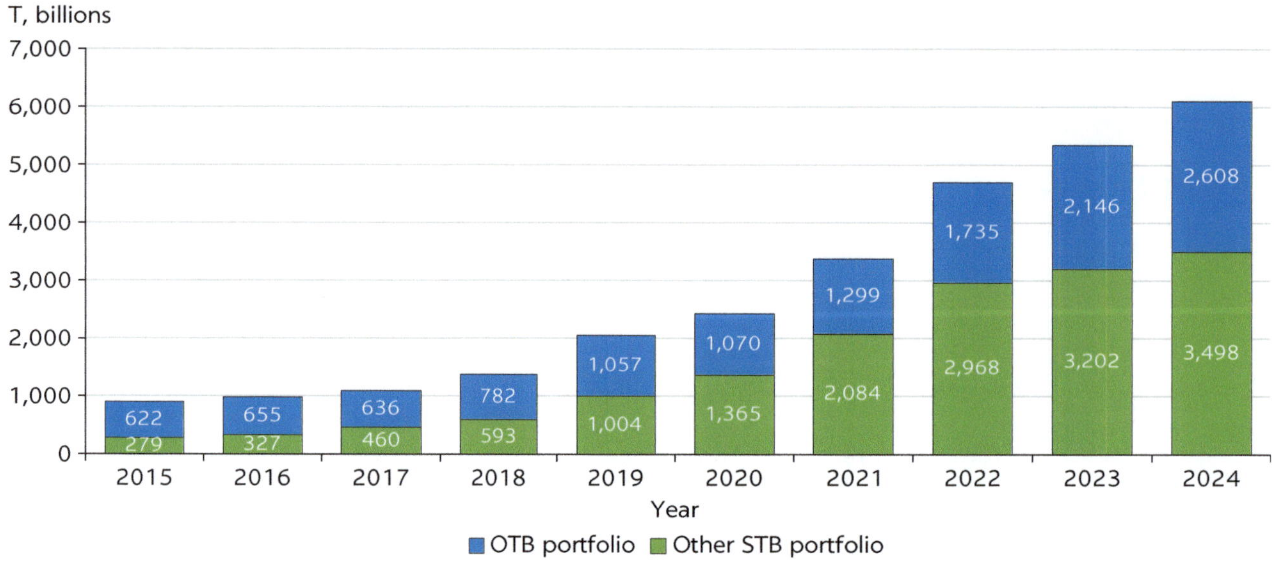

Sources: Original figure for this publication using data from NBK (2026) and OTB (2024a, 2024b, n.d.).
Note: NBK = National Bank of Kazakhstan; OTB = Otbasy Bank; STB = second-tier bank.

MORTGAGE PRODUCTS

As mentioned earlier, Kazakhstan's housing finance landscape includes two distinct groups of products: mortgages from OTB's S&L program and mortgages from other banks, most of which are market priced. Subsidized loans under the NBK 7-20-25 program are also extended by STBs. These options are illustrated in table 2.1.

Generally, loan-underwriting terms appear sound, although certain products could present potential risks. Mortgages are originated in local currency only and at reasonable terms, including a level pay structure and prudent down-payment requirements. The aggregate mortgage portfolio performs well, with NPLs below 1 percent. Lenders also offer loans for unfinished (off-plan) properties sold by developers who are financed through the same lenders' corporate loan portfolios. Interest rates and monthly payments for such loans are lower than for mortgages for completed dwellings. Because such developer-linked loans have lower monthly payments than ordinary market-priced mortgages, they are affordable for the top-two income deciles (20 percent of the population), whereas market-priced loans are affordable only for applicants from the top income decile (10 percent of the population).

However, the reduced interest rate for such developer-linked loans comes at a price, usually in the form of a higher property price (refer to box 2.1 for details).

TABLE 2.1 Prevailing housing finance products, 2024 originations

	LOAN TERM (MONTHS)	INTEREST RATE (% PER YEAR)	LTV (%)	AVERAGE LOAN AMOUNT (T MILLION)	NUMBER OF LOANS AND MARKET SHARE[a]	NOTES
Classic market-priced mortgages from banks	Up to 240	~20	70–85	17+	n.a.	No subsidy, low affordability (10%); clients are in the top decile by income
Developer-linked market-priced mortgages from banks	Up to 240	~15	70–85	17+	n.a	No subsidy, inflated property price, off-plan purchase, low affordability (20%); clients are in the top-two deciles by income
Subsidized mortgages under 7-20-25 NBK program	Up to 300	7	80	17	6,000 or 5%	Annual program size T 100 billion, new construction only
OTB S&L products	Up to 240	6–9	100	15	60,000 or 45%	Untargeted S&L, low affordability (10%)
	Up to 240	2–5	100	15	20,000 or 15%	Targeted programs for vulnerable and low-income households, good affordability (60%)

Sources: Original table for this publication using data from NBK (2025), OTB, and World Bank Group calculations from staff interviews with OTB, NBK, and STBs.
Note: LTV = loan-to-value ratio; n.a. = not applicable; NBK = National Bank of Kazakhstan; OTB = Otbasy Bank; S&L = savings and loan; STBs = second-tier banks.
a. Estimated total number of originations of about 130,000 loans calculated based on the total 2024 originations of T 2,023 billion and average loan amount of about T 15 million.

Digitization of mortgage lending has been accelerating in Kazakhstan as part of the advanced digitization of financial services in the country. For example, Freedom Bank's creation of a seamless digital mortgage-lending process is a testament to both the lender's ingenuity and the sophisticated legal and market infrastructure of the retail housing market. This market-first initiative allows for a fully remote borrower–lender relationship, where application, underwriting, loan disbursement, and other mortgage issuance steps are handled online. This process is made possible not only by the advanced digitization of some mortgage lenders but also by equally impressive online capabilities within the property registration system and by borrowers' familiarity and comfort with mobile and online tools, even in the context of a transaction as significant as a house purchase.

Other banks have yet to achieve the same level of digitalization, but the process of obtaining a mortgage from any lender is streamlined and convenient for applicants. The impact on housing affordability of fully digitizing the lending process, however, is likely negligible.

Box 2.1

Inflated-price, lower-rate mechanism used by developers and lenders

By raising property prices above their true market value, lenders can offer a lower nominal rate while still earning the same present value (PV) return, allowing them to protect their income while appearing to make loans more affordable. Such schemes are relatively common globally and involve collusion between the lender and the property developer; the latter raises the property price above market levels, and the former reduces the mortgage interest rate so that the borrower sees lower monthly payments, even as the lender maintains the desired interest income on the PV basis. For example, the monthly payment for an average non–Otbasy Bank loan of T 17 million (~US$33,000) for 15 years at 20 percent per year would be about T 300,000, and the PV of lender income would be T 14.3 million.

However, if the property price is increased by 20 percent to T 20.4 million and the interest rate is lowered to 14 percent per year, the monthly payment would be lower, at T 271,000—but the lender's interest income would remain practically the same on the PV basis.

Such products likely pose consumer protection, market, and credit risks for borrowers and lenders in the event of negative or flat house price appreciation (HPA) (a situation in which borrowers seeking to sell their homes find that the "real" price is lower than they originally paid). In addition, a significant volume of transactions at artificially inflated prices could skew market-wide statistics, creating a misleading impression of a positive HPA.

Making Islamic housing finance products available could potentially support greater financial inclusion and affordability.[3] The introduction of such products—both lease and purchase types—is being discussed by sector stakeholders and will require a sharia-specific statutory and regulatory framework for consumer protection.[4] It will also require assessing the potential impact of such products on affordability. It is important not to misrepresent or falsely advertise such loans as having "zero interest," as lenders may be motivated to do amid high mortgage rates. The implied interest paid to the lender in the form of "profit" would need to be properly disclosed to borrowers in a way directly comparable to the disclosure of information about conventional mortgages, likely under specific regulation by the Agency of the Republic of Kazakhstan for Regulation and Development of Financial Market (ARDFM). Broadly, significant efforts are needed to ensure that Islamic finance borrowers understand the specific risks and responsibilities associated with those products. Should Islamic housing finance portfolios grow to a meaningful size, specific capital market instruments ("sukuk") may become viable and require appropriate legal and regulatory development as well.

Mortgage credit risk protection mechanisms—specifically mortgage insurance (MI) and mortgage guarantees (MGs)—are absent, even though they may be relevant to deepening the market for lower-income borrowers, those without a sufficient down payment, and those with informal income sources. Classical MI products may provide down-payment support and be a highly efficient subsidy mechanism for young families or others without the capacity for a significant down payment, whereas MG solutions may facilitate market deepening for borrowers with low and informal incomes; they are an efficient instrument for subsidy transmission for such borrowers and for socially vulnerable borrowers. The fiscal efficiency of these solutions arises from the higher multiplier of private capital relative to public capital. Specifically, assuming that MI and MGs are capitalized at least in part by budgetary resources, a prudent capital-to-risk ratio is around 1:10–12. That is, for every T 1 of budget resources, there would be T 10–12 of private financial capital.

Providing public support for premium payments—for example, covering part of borrowers' MI premiums or MG fees—offers another channel through which subsidies can reach targeted households. This type of support can also generate a high subsidy multiplier, because a relatively small public contribution can unlock much larger volumes of private lending by reducing credit risk, lowering required up-front payments, and thus making mortgages more affordable.[5]

There are several legal and regulatory considerations for MI and MGs:

- Product mandate and scope, including decisions on whether MI and MGs are mandatory (for example, required for a loan-to-value [LTV] ratio above a certain threshold, for certain subsidized programs, or for lender eligibility) or optional, and decisions on whether MI or an MG is applicable at the loan level, at the pool level, or as portfolio credit enhancement
- Eligibility and underwriting standards, including decisions on statutory or regulatory definitions of eligible collateral, borrower affordability tests, documentation rules, maximum LTV and debt-to-income ratios, property valuation standards, and exclusions (for example, investor or second homes, certain property types)
- Coverage and claims framework, including decisions on minimum and maximum coverage percentages by LTV band, first-loss versus pro rata loss sharing, cure periods, timelines for claim submission and payment, dispute mechanisms, and rules on rescission or denial
- Prudential and accounting treatment, including decisions on treatment of guaranteed and insured loans under bank capital rules (for example, risk weight substitution or credit risk mitigation [CRM] recognition), operational requirements to obtain capital relief (legal enforceability, direct claim rights, and no material exclusions), provisioning expectations, and concentration limits
- Insurer and guarantor regulation and solvency, including decisions on licensing, capital and reserve requirements, stress testing, investment limits, reinsurance rules, and supervisory powers (including intervention and resolution)

- Counterparty and governance controls, including decisions on approved insurer lists, exposure limits to a single guarantor, board independence and best-practice risk governance for public guarantee funds, and transparency on contingent liabilities when government backed
- Consumer and market conduct safeguards, including decisions on guarantee or insurance premium disclosure, payment by borrower or lender, cancellation and refund rules, servicing standards, and controls on tied selling (so that the MI or MG regime protects lenders prudentially and remains credible, predictable, and enforceable across the credit cycle).

Kazakhstan has a history of using MI instruments. Significant legal and regulatory developments regarding MI and MGs since the 2008–09 global financial crisis warrant highlighting. Specifically, MI and MG frameworks have been tightened in two reinforcing directions: (1) greater insurer and guarantor resilience and (2) claims certainty, as well as more prescriptive prudential recognition of credit protection.

On the resilience side, the crisis exposed the possibility that mortgage insurers could be undercapitalized for a severe housing downturn and, under stress, might not fully pay claims. In response, regulators (for example, the US Federal Housing Finance Agency overseeing the government-sponsored enterprises) required aligned eligibility standards to ensure that approved MI products demonstrated the financial and operational capacity to withstand a severe downturn. This requirement underwent major revisions in 2015 and again in 2018 in the United States. On the prudential regulatory side, Basel post-crisis reforms put greater emphasis on CRM enforceability and comparability (for example, through targeted fixes and clarified CRM implementation), reflecting lessons about model risk and inconsistent recognition of mitigants.

In practice, the prudential considerations have contributed to an observable regulatory and market preference for guarantee-like structures (including "mortgage guarantee insurance" structured to behave like a guarantee). This has occurred for two reasons: first, because capital relief frameworks are anchored in "eligible guarantees"—and insurance can receive similar recognition only if it satisfies multiple "guarantee-like" elements (for example, written form, unconditionality, direct claim, limits on unilateral cancellation, legal enforceability, or timely payment without first suing the borrower); and second, because insurers are not always treated as "eligible guarantors" or do not deliver meaningful risk weight substitution under banking capital rules. Kazakhstan can learn from these global developments as well as from its own past experiences with MG loan schemes (refer to box 2.2).

Box 2.2

Kazakhstan's Mortgage Loan Guarantee Fund: Evolution, lessons, and current policy relevance

Kazakhstan has prior institutional experience with a dedicated mortgage credit risk guarantee facility through the Kazakhstan Mortgage Loan Guarantee Fund (KLGF; called AO Казахстанский фонд гарантирования ипотечных кредитов [КЗГИК] in Kazakhstan). KLGF was established in 2003 under National Bank of Kazakhstan framework decisions and early financial sector development architecture. The fund's core concept was to share and mitigate mortgage credit risk, thereby enabling lenders to prudently expand mortgage access. Relevant program documentation and supervisory materials describe a guarantee approach designed to absorb a defined portion of risk and enable higher-risk lending within controlled parameters. Over time, the institution was reconfigured and its functions consolidated. In 2016, the successor vehicle, the Housing Construction Guarantee Fund (called AO Фонд гарантирования жилищного строительства [ФГЖС] in Kazakhstan), was formed, and in 2020–21, it was merged into the Kazakhstan Housing Company as part of Baiterek's housing sector consolidation.

The KLGF design matters for today's policy agenda because it offers a practical precedent for a modern mortgage insurance (MI) or mortgage guarantee (MG) facility aimed at low- and irregular-income (including informal) borrowers and at those without a sufficient down payment. KLGF products were intended to ensure exposure above a policy threshold of around a 70 percent loan-to-value (LTV) ratio, which is exactly the type of credit enhancement that can unlock prudent high-LTV/low-down-payment products when paired with strong underwriting, standardized documentation, and disciplined risk management. Reintroducing a fit-for-purpose facility—potentially with a public–private structure, risk-based pricing, and explicit loss-sharing and risk retention rules—would allow lenders to extend targeted products to underserved segments (including via alternative income verification and staged or step-up pathways), while keeping credit standards transparent and enforceable.

Finally, an MI or MG facility is also an enabler of capital markets. By providing credible, rule-based credit enhancement (and by promoting standardization of origination, servicing, data, and disclosure), such a facility can materially strengthen the investability of mortgage pools. It can also support the development of covered bonds, mortgage-backed securities, and other refinancing channels—especially in a context where investor confidence, prudential treatment, and data transparency are decisive. Kazakhstan's earlier experience with KLGF demonstrates that the country has already tested the institutional logic of risk sharing to expand access. The proposed reintroduction would update that logic to reflect current priorities: inclusive mortgage products, resilient risk management, and scalable mortgage-backed capital market funding.

GOVERNMENT SUPPORT PROGRAMS FOR HOUSING FINANCE AND THEIR IMPACT

Kazakhstan dedicates substantial public resources to housing subsidies, yet the effectiveness and targeting of these expenditures remain below potential, limiting their impact on housing affordability. In 2024, housing subsidies in

Kazakhstan (including for housing finance) totaled at least T 950 billion (~US$2 billion) (Prime Minister of the Republic of Kazakhstan 2024; Trend News Agency 2024), representing approximately 0.7 percent of gross domestic product (GDP). This figure aligns with the Organisation for Economic Co-operation and Development (OECD) average of about 1 percent and indicates a reasonable level of public support.[6] At the same time, the impact of the subsidy volume on housing affordability remains limited due to suboptimal targeting and a suboptimal monitoring and evaluation (M&E) system.

The government intervenes throughout the entire housing market value chain, from construction to mortgage finance. Two Baiterek Holding subsidiaries, KHC and OTB, are explicitly designated to support housing construction and finance housing purchases through guarantees and subsidized loans that aim to improve housing affordability. In addition, NBK has been running a dedicated mortgage subsidy program since 2018, although this is planned to be phased out.

The mortgage-lending sector has been significantly influenced by state interventions. For example, in 2021, following the government's decision to allow individuals to use pension savings to improve housing conditions, mortgage loans soared by 37.7 percent (Ministry of Justice, Institute of Legislation and Legal Information 2021). Another instance of state intervention that notably impacted market dynamics was the NBK's new round of financing for the 7-20-25 program, which contributed to a 42.6 percent increase in mortgage loans in 2022 (National Bank of Kazakhstan 2025). Subsequently, the government and NBK implemented measures to tighten the eligibility criteria of their support programs and reduce financing to prevent market distortions. As a result, in 2023 and 2024, mortgage loans experienced a more moderate annual growth rate of 14 percent, and by end-2025, they accounted for approximately 17 percent of total loans.[7]

Explicit subsidies

Explicit subsidies for public housing finance primarily consist of support for OTB members in the form of a deposit premium and a reduced lending rate under targeted state programs and NBK's 7-20-25 program. The rather small 7-20-25 program—T 100 billion annually, or 5 percent of yearly originations—carries a reduced annual interest rate of 7 percent, about one-third of the current market-based rate. The number of benefiting households is small, at about 6,000 per year.[8] Public subsidies for the OTB's S&L scheme illustrate the significant volume of government involvement in the mortgage market—and the opportunity to increase its impact. As discussed later, by end-2025, OTB was the sole operator and the transmission vehicle for several public housing finance support (subsidy) programs that target households with certain socioeconomic characteristics.[9]

Under the first type of subsidy for public housing finance, OTB members benefit from an annual budgetary deposit premium. This premium is not linked to the monetary policy rate (or the evolving cost of capital in the economy) and, in effect, is a down-payment subsidy that accrues over time to maintain a deposit to be used when taking a loan from OTB. In financial terms, the per-member and aggregate amounts of the S&L premium are fairly significant: The aggregate premium has been over T 360 billion (over US$700 million) during the past 5 years, averaging T 72 billion (US$140 million) annually.

Under the second type of subsidy, the budget subsidizes OTB debt issuance by paying a portion of the coupon over 7 percent a year on OTB bonds. So, in effect, state budget co-pays the difference between the actual coupon rate of OTB bonds (which is close to the NBK base rate) and 7 percent, which pays OTB (Ministry of Justice, Institute of Legislation and Legal Information 2024). The amount is estimated to be about T 33 billion (just under US$65 million) in 2025. The support will last for as long as the bonds remain outstanding, and it may increase if there are new OTB bond placements at similarly subsidized terms.

Note that the relative subsidy efficiency of OTB public support is higher than that of the NBK 7-20-25 program.[10] With a similar annual volume of about T 100 billion (US$195 million), OTB originates over 80,000 loans, compared to fewer than 6,000 extended under the 7-20-25 program. Moreover, good global practices suggest that subsidized public financial capital should be crowding in (leveraging) funding from private sources. Both OTB and NBK subsidies do not crowd in private resources—they use only public capital.

In addition, the subsidy targeting is distorted because about 50 percent of OTB mortgages are affordable only for families in the top income decile (top 10 percent of families), who presumably do not need public support. Indeed, judging by their monthly payment capacity, they have the means to obtain an unsubsidized mortgage from a private lender. The NBK subsidy also does not have income eligibility criteria for borrowers.

Impact of Otbasy Bank's subsidized loans on other second-tier banks' lending

OTB has played a central role in expanding access to affordable housing finance through targeted subsidized mortgage programs. Box 2.3 examines how this expansion affects mortgage lending by other commercial banks. Figure 2.2 shows that the share of OTB's subsidized mortgages has increased markedly over the past decade, reflecting its expanding role in Kazakhstan's housing finance market.

Box 2.3

Impact of Otbasy Bank's subsidized mortgages on private sector mortgage lending

An analysis was undertaken to understand how subsidized mortgages offered by Otbasy Bank (OTB) affect private sector mortgage lending. The analysis uses quarterly regional mortgage issuance data from 2015 to 2025, encompassing 19 regions (excluding newly established regions due to limited historical data). The empirical model relates the growth of other banks' mortgage lending to changes in OTB's lending and its prior market share:

$$\Delta \ln(\text{Other Loan}_{rt}) = \beta_1 \Delta \ln(\text{Otbasy Loan}_{rt}) + \beta_2 \ln(\text{Otbasy Share}_{r,t-1}) + \beta_3[\Delta \ln(\text{Otbasy Loan}_{rt}) \times \ln(\text{Otbasy Share}_{r,t-1})] + X_{rt}\gamma + \alpha_r + \tau_t + \epsilon_{rt} \quad \text{(Eq. B2.3.1)}$$

The interaction term captures whether the effect of new OTB lending differs in regions where the bank already holds a larger market share. Because the model is expressed in log changes, the coefficients can be interpreted as elasticities—showing how other banks' mortgage lending responds, in percentage terms, to changes in OTB's lending, considering its existing market share. The specification controls for regional employment, income, housing prices, and new housing supply, along with region and time fixed effects and region-specific trends.

The regression results show a strongly negative interaction term: A 1 percent increase in OTB's lending reduces other banks' mortgage loan growth by about 0.28 percent for each log point increase in OTB's lagged market share. This indicates that crowding out is more pronounced in regions where OTB is already more dominant, even though increases in the bank's lending may coincide with stronger overall mortgage demand.

The dynamic estimates in figure B2.3.1 plot the projected effect of this interaction term up to 12 quarters ahead using a local projections framework. The coefficients are significantly negative in the short run, confirming an immediate substitution effect when OTB expands lending in markets where it already has a substantial presence. As the projection horizon widens, the interaction effect declines in magnitude and becomes statistically indistinguishable from zero, suggesting that the influence of OTB's prior market share on other banks' lending is temporary rather than persistent.

Overall, the results indicate that OTB's subsidized mortgage programs crowd out commercial banks' mortgage lending, with stronger effects in regions where OTB already holds a larger market share. However, the weakening of the dynamic coefficients over time implies that this substitution does not persist and does not lead to long-run structural displacement of private lenders. Instead, the market appears to be adjusting as the initial impact fades out. However, any subsequent increases in OTB lending send another short-term crowding-out shock to the private mortgage market. These findings underscore the importance of designing housing finance interventions that mitigate short-term disruptions and help mobilize private capital for the deepening of Kazakhstan's mortgage market.

continued

Box 2.3, Impact of Otbasy Bank's subsidized mortgages on private sector mortgage lending *(continued)*

FIGURE B2.3.1

Dynamic effects of the Otbasy program launches on other banks' lending

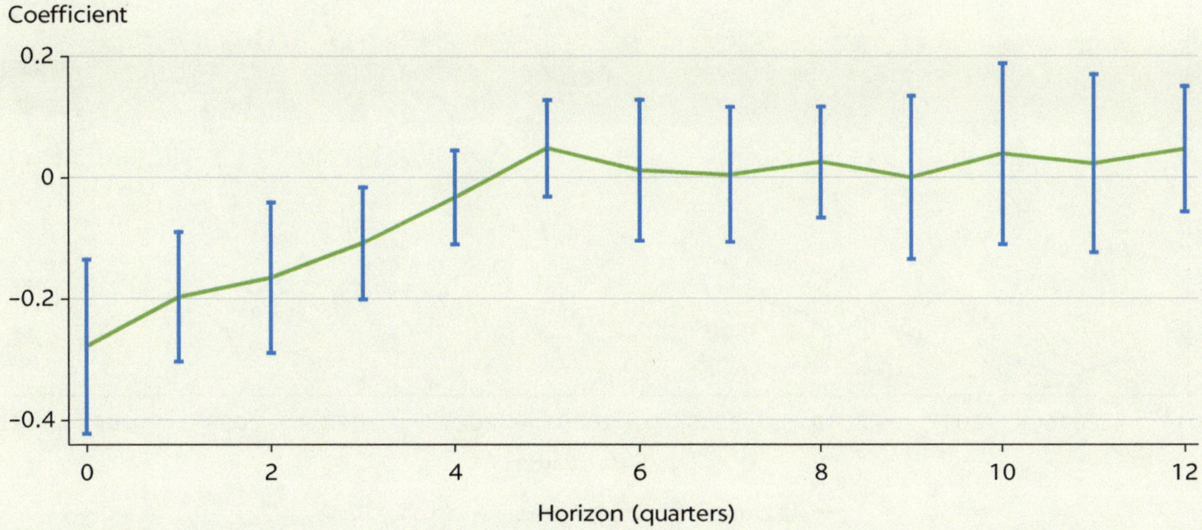

Source: World Bank calculations.

These preliminary results are being elaborated in a more comprehensive analysis (Mao and Melecky, forthcoming), which uses a staggered treatment specification to shed more light on OTB subsidized mortgage programs' crowding out private bank mortgage activity and related intertemporal dynamics.

Suggested subsidy logic, impact metrics, and monitoring and evaluation

Kazakhstan's public support programs would benefit from significantly improved targeting and M&E systems to ensure that subsidies deliver real additionality rather than simply expanding intermediated volumes. The M&E of housing finance subsidies in Kazakhstan is currently limited, fragmented, and mostly focused on tracking pre-set quantitative indicators and intermediated volumes; it does not assess socioeconomic impacts or qualitative aspects. Ultimately, M&E systems for public support programs (and for the development finance institutions administering them, such as KHC and OTB) should aim to measure additionality. Measuring performance by looking at intermediated resources could incentivize portfolio growth and competition with private providers rather than addressing market failures, catering to underserved segments, and crowding in private capital to the mortgage market. Box 2.3 details the current effect of OTB mortgage programs on private bank participation in the mortgage loan market.

FIGURE 2.2

Mortgage-lending trends, 2015–25: Loan issuance volumes (T, billions)

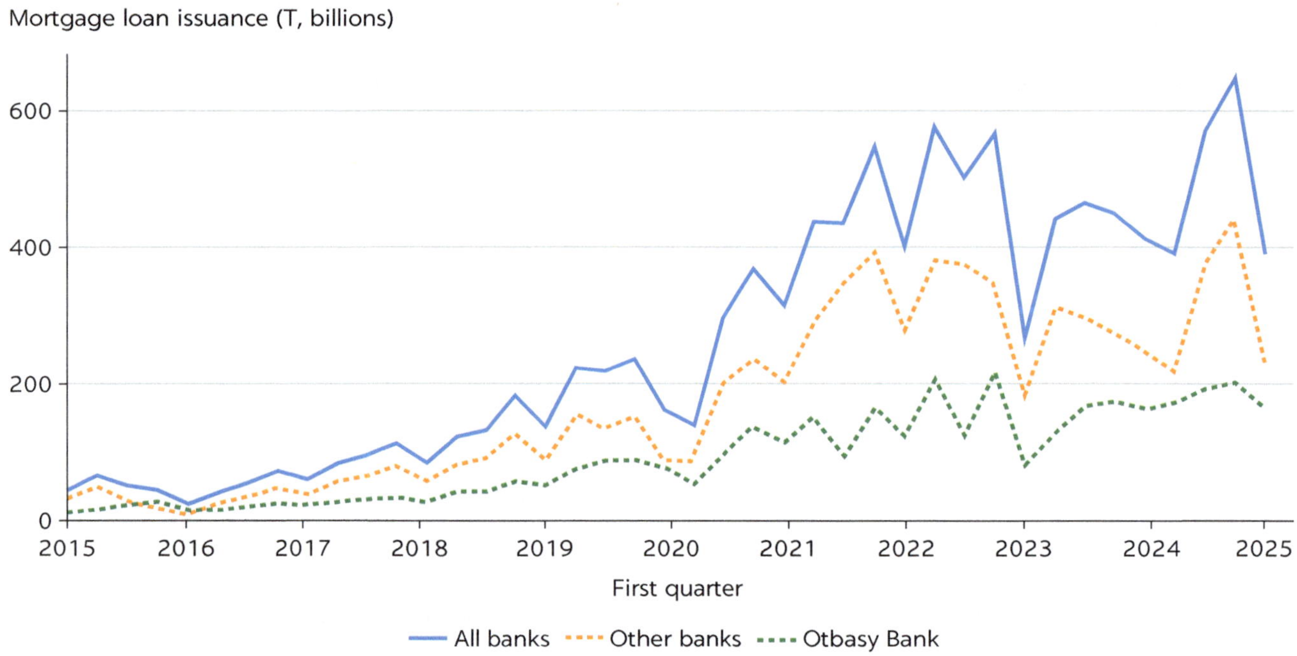

Sources: National Bank of Kazakhstan (2025) and Otbasy Bank (n.d.).

Key principles of effective subsidy M&E are briefly discussed as follows:

- The subsidy's goal is to **increase affordability.**[11] That is, the goal is to enable families from lower-income deciles to obtain homes by using available housing finance solutions. As the key instrument for families seeking to obtain homes, housing finance is socially important. Policy makers deem it necessary to support those financially unable to purchase or sustain a proper dwelling or to access housing finance. Subsidies can be direct, that is, explicitly apparent to the beneficiary in financial terms, or indirect, usually taking the form of legal and regulatory preferences for stakeholders in the housing finance sector.
- Thus, the **subsidy intent** is to financially support lower-income families in obtaining mortgage finance—either directly by transferring monies to beneficiaries or indirectly by designing and implementing loan products with preferential terms, often in the form of a lower-than-market interest rate.
- The critical public support metric is **targeting,** that is, making sure that budgetary resources are, in fact, reaching those the policy maker intends to support and are not captured by other borrowers. This is achieved by setting and verifying **robust criteria for beneficiary eligibility,** typically including income level, eligible property price, and maximum loan amount. Common population segments targeted for subsidies include families with low or informal income (or otherwise in disadvantaged circumstances), as well as some social groups, such as doctors and public employees, as part of professional incentives.

- Broadly, subsidies should be **targeted toward borrowers from lower- and middle-income deciles** (for example, deciles 1–6), keeping in mind that homeownership is likely not feasible for the very poor population, who may require other solutions, such as rental subsidies or social housing.
- Once robust targeting is achieved and monitored, **subsidy effectiveness** needs to be measured. This metric deals with how meaningful the support is in helping families obtain housing finance relative to their needs. That is, effectiveness measures the degree to which the subsidy amount and distribution mechanisms actually ease access to mortgages.
- **Subsidy efficiency**—the achievement of subsidy goals with the minimum of fiscal and other resources—can be expressed by the number of beneficiaries impacted for a given volume of support. The higher the number, the more efficient the subsidy is. Typically, this metric is increased by combining public and private financial capital. For example, a down-payment subsidy enables borrowers to obtain a market-priced mortgage from a lender. A multiplier denotes the inverse of the ratio between public and private funding. Ceteris paribus, the higher the multiplier (or the smaller the share of the public funding), the better. Some financial mechanisms allow for very high multipliers, for example, publicly capitalized credit insurance or guarantee facilities, where each T 1 of capital would plausibly lead to T 15–18 of the mortgage portfolio covered. A down-payment subsidy of 10–20 percent of the loan amount has a multiplier of 5–10, which is also reasonably high.
- **Subsidy impact** is measured in terms of affordability increase or mortgage market deepening, where housing finance becomes a viable homeownership tool for lower-income families (families in lower deciles of the income distribution).
- **Subsidy transmission** takes many forms, such as being institutionalized in a state-owned enterprise or public-private partnership format. Typical product-level subsidy mechanics include lower mortgage interest rates; borrower down-payment support; and mortgage insurance, guarantees, or cofinancing.
- To ensure **fairness in subsidy allocation,** beneficiary eligibility criteria and product mechanics should allow the flow of the subsidy only to those families who need it. For example, eligibility could be once per lifetime, and collateralized property sales could be restricted. In practice, the loan agreement could contain a clause that expressly provides for the lender's consent for any transactions with the apartment and either prohibits full loan prepayment for a certain period of time or imposes significant penalties for it.
- Good global practices include the following:
  - Avoiding market distortion by robustly targeting beneficiaries
  - Supporting the borrower and not the developer
  - Supporting the down payment and not the interest rate
  - Limiting subsidy access to once per lifetime
  - Using significant private capital bail-in to achieve a high private-to-public capital multiplier.

NOTES

1. The determination of increased market rates uses the NBK base rate as a proxy; this rate increased from 9 percent at year-end 2020 to 16.5 percent as of 2025.
2. Based on Kazakhstan Housing Company (2024) and World Bank Group calculations.
3. Traditional Islamic housing finance products include ijara (property lease from the lender-lessor to the borrower-lessee with the title conveyed to the latter at lease end), murabaha (immediate property resale transaction from the lender to the borrower at the higher price), and musharaka (a joint property purchase with the title gradually transitioning to the borrower over the life of the loan). Overall, for these types of financial arrangements, it is important to create the perception that there are no interest payments, so loans nominally do not have an interest rate, but lender profit is expressed in the price of the property itself. Specific products and their details vary by country.
4. One possibility being discussed is introducing "Islamic windows" in traditional banks to offer sharia-compliant financial products, including Islamic mortgages.
5. For discussion of subsidy efficiency and other metrics, refer to the "Explicit Subsidies" section.
6. The OECD average is about 1 percent relative to GDP. Refer to the OECD Affordable Housing Database at https://www.oecd.org/en/data/datasets/oecd-affordable-housing-database.html and the OECD Social Expenditure Database at https://www.oecd.org/en/data/datasets/social-expenditure-database-socx.html. Precise numbers are challenging to ascertain because not all public support is reported, and some duplications can occur. Individual country numbers can vary significantly.
7. Growth rates of loans and other indicators of the banking system are obtained from monthly ARDFM publications; refer to ARDFM, "Banking Sector (Performance of Financial Sector)," https://www.gov.kz/memleket/entities/ardfm/press/article/details/72350?lang=en.
8. According to NBK, the current portfolio outstanding of the 7-20-25 program is T 1.09 trillion (about US$2 billion), with 79,000 loans. This brings the average loan size to about T 13.5 million. According to the Kazakhstan Housing Company (2024), program originations in 2024 numbered 5,900 loans with an average loan amount of T 17 million.
9. For details, refer to chapter 3.
10. The comparison is valid notwithstanding different sources of the subsidy; while the Government of Kazakhstan needs either to borrow financial capital or to spend fiscal resources, NBK creates money directly for its 7-20-25 program. Note that, in simple terms, "efficiency" measures how many beneficiaries are affected by the subsidy volume on margin. Ordinarily, efficiency is increased by requiring private financial capital involvement, such as occurs when there is down-payment support from the budget, but the mortgage itself is originated by a private bank.
11. Refer to chapter 3 for a discussion of affordability.

REFERENCES

Kazakhstan Housing Company. 2024. "Mortgage Lending in the Republic of Kazakhstan: Overview for 2024" [in Russian]. https://khc.kz/upload/sprint.editor/057/bf1279nuic8nx35wyabgp66jahg6qu4u.pdf.

Mao, C., and M. Melecky. Forthcoming. "Do Subsidized Mortgages Crowd Out Private Lending?" World Bank.

Ministry of Justice, Institute of Legislation and Legal Information. 2021. "On Approval of the Rules for the Use of Lump-Sum Pension Payments to Improve Housing Conditions in Accordance with the Legislation of the Republic of Kazakhstan" [in Russian]. Order of the Minister of Industry and Infrastructural Development of the Republic of Kazakhstan, No. 24. https://adilet.zan.kz/rus/docs/V2100022100.

Ministry of Justice, Institute of Legislation and Legal Information. 2024. "On Approval of the Rules for Subsidizing the Coupon Interest Rate on Bonds Issued by the Issuer for Further Issuance of Housing Mortgage Loans for the Purpose of Improving Housing Conditions in Accordance with the Legislation of the Republic of Kazakhstan" [in Russian]. Order of the Minister of Industry and Construction of the Republic of Kazakhstan, No. 190. https://adilet.zan.kz/rus/docs/V2400034409.

National Bank of Kazakhstan. 2025. "'7-20-25' Programs" [in Russian]. https://nationalbank.kz/ru/news/ipotechnoe-kreditovanie-po-programme-72025/6225.

Otbasy Bank. 2024a. "Key Events of the Reporting Year." https://hcsbk.kz/about-the-bank/reporting/go-2024/en/klyucheve-sobtiya-otchetnogo-goda.html.

Otbasy Bank. 2024b. "Key Sustainability Events in 2024." https://hcsbk.kz/about-the-bank/reporting/our-2024/en/klyucheve-sobtiya-v-oblasti-ustochivogo-razvitiya-v-2024-godu.html.

Otbasy Bank. n.d. "Annual Reports." https://hcsbk.kz/en/about-the-bank/reporting/.

Prime Minister of the Republic of Kazakhstan. 2024. "Support for Housing Construction at Expense of Kazakhstan Housing Company JSC Totalled 640.3 Billion Tenge." December 10, 2024. https://primeminister.kz/en/news/support-for-housing-construction-at-expense-of-kazakhstan-housing-company-jsc-totalled-6403-billion-tenge-29450.

Trend News Agency. 2024. "Kazakhstan Reveals Allocations for Housing Construction in 2024." April 23, 2024. https://www.trend.az/casia/kazakhstan/3889769.html.

3 Housing Affordability

METHODOLOGY

This report uses a robust, policy-oriented definition of *housing affordability:* the percentage of the population by income that can afford to obtain a suitable dwelling using prevailing housing finance solutions.[1] In an efficient market, the median (50 percent) of households by income can prudently obtain a home at the median price. Moreover, in such a market, subsidies are targeted to households with incomes below the median. Typically, affordability is measured without public support programs. However, as Kazakhstan's housing finance ecosystem is still developing, affordability calculations in this report include all available mortgage products, including the subsidized ones discussed in chapter 2.

This approach to measuring affordability is closely aligned with sound global practice. For example, the approach of the US National Association of Realtors includes the core components (a representative home price, a representative mortgage product, and an underwriting affordability constraint) in an affordability index; refer to more details in box 3.1.

This report uses a similar logic but calculates not an index but a percentage of households by income that can afford a median-priced home. This distributional approach is more policy focused as it answers a question central to housing policy: What percentage of households by income can afford homes under current market conditions? This number is also directly comparable across regions, subsidy policy levers, and mortgage-underwriting assumptions.

A typical situation in many developing markets is that only high-income households (those at the top of the income distribution) have the means to improve their housing conditions by using prevailing mortgage products. The key policy objective, therefore, is to increase affordability—that is, to increase the number of households that can afford a new home using available housing finance solutions. Changes in mortgage products, including subsidized ones,

Box 3.1

The NAR Housing Affordability Index

The US National Association of Realtors (NAR) Housing Affordability Index asks a simple question: Can a "typical" (median-income) family qualify for a conventional mortgage on a "typical" (median-priced) existing single-family home?

NAR uses the median existing-home price from its monthly survey, the median family income from Census data (with projections used after 2017, when needed), and an effective mortgage rate (rate on loans closed, including amortized fees). It then computes the monthly principal and interest (P&I) payment for an 80 percent loan (20 percent down payment) on a 30-year fixed-rate mortgage and derives the qualifying income assuming P&I equals 25 percent of gross income (qualifying income = monthly P&I × 4 × 12, meaning that one-quarter of the household income should be allocated to paying off the mortgage, expressed in annual terms).

An index value of 100 means the median-income family has exactly the income needed to qualify; above 100 means more than enough, and below 100 means not enough. In the context of this report, the NAR Housing Affordability Index of 100 would mean balanced market conditions, that is, 50 percent of families can afford a mortgage.

Source: NAR, "Methodology: Housing Affordability Index," https://www.nar.realtor/research-and-statistics/housing-statistics/housing-affordability-index/methodology.

can be designed and implemented faster than household income levels, housing supply, and house prices can evolve. Therefore, assessing housing affordability provides timely guidance for housing finance policy makers.

Specifically, the affordability calculation in this report maps monthly payments for a typical mortgage using the interest rate, loan term, and loan amount to households by income deciles. Thus, estimating affordability is a three-step process that involves (1) obtaining income distribution information, (2) identifying the prevailing financial options available to borrowers, and (3) combining the two. About half of households in the top-two income deciles (roughly 4 million people) reside in three metropolitan statistical areas (MSAs)—Almaty, Astana, and Shymkent (National Statistical Bureau, Agency for Strategic Planning and Reforms 2025). This statistic aligns well with data showing that over 50 percent of mortgage loans are issued in these MSAs.

Housing affordability is an objective, policy-oriented indicator that directly illustrates not only how many families have the opportunity to address their housing needs but also who these families are in terms of income. Refer to box 3.2 for an illustrative application to regions of the United States.

Box 3.2

Regional affordability in the United States

To illustrate housing affordability in one of the most advanced housing finance markets globally—that of the United States—this box examines regional US affordability.

Key inputs include the following:

- *Household income.* Census Current Population Survey tables reporting household "total money income" (not income per person)[a]
- *Home prices.* National Association of Realtors October 2025 median existing-home prices by region[b]
- *Mortgage.* 30-year fixed, 6.25 percent interest rate, 80 percent loan-to-value (LTV) ratio
- *Property tax.* State effective tax rates, averaged to Census regions (simple unweighted average across states in each region)[c]
- *Insurance.* Average premiums by state for US$300,000 dwelling coverage, averaged within regions and scaled linearly[d]
- *Underwriting constraints.* These constraints include the following:
    - *Housing-only cap:* 30 percent of gross income (principal, interest, taxes, insurance [PITI])[e]
    - *Back-end (net) debt-to-income (DTI) ratio cap:* 35 percent
    - *7 percent of income reserved for other debts,* so DTI is effectively capped at 28 percent.

The results of applying affordability calculations are shown in table B3.2.1. The table highlights stark regional disparities in housing affordability across the United States. The West and Northeast face the highest house prices and income thresholds, resulting in the lowest shares of households qualifying for a median-priced home. In contrast, the Midwest remains the most affordable region, with lower PITI payments and nearly half of households meeting standard mortgage qualification criteria under typical DTI and LTV assumptions.

TABLE B3.2.1 Housing affordability and income qualification, by US region

US REGION	MEDIAN HOUSE PRICE (US$)	ESTIMATED MONTHLY PITI (US$)	HOUSEHOLD ANNUAL INCOME NEEDED TO QUALIFY (US$)	HOUSEHOLDS THAT QUALIFY (%)
Northeast	504,000	3,200	137,000	34
Midwest	320,000	2,200	93,000	45
South	360,000	2,300	99,000	40
West	630,000	3,800	161,000	27

Source: Original table for this publication.
Note: NAR = National Association of Realtors; PITI = principal, interest, taxes, insurance; US = United States. Values are rounded for readability.
a. Income distribution tables from Current Population Survey in US Census Bureau, "HINC-01: Selected Characteristics of Households by Total Money Income (percentiles, etc.)," https://www.census.gov/data/tables/time-series/demo/income-poverty/cps-hinc/hinc-01.html.
b. NAR 2025. The article reports that the October 2025 median existing-home price was US$415,200 and provides regional median prices, including the Northeast, US$503,700; the Midwest, US$319,500; the South, US$362,300; and the West, US$628,500.
c. Bankrate 2025 (table for tax year 2024, sourced from ATTOM Data Solutions).
d. Insurance.com, "Average Homeowners' Insurance Rates by State," updated Dec 4, 2025, https://www.insurance.com/home-and-renters-insurance/home-insurance-basics/average-homeowners-insurance-rates-by-state (state table for $300,000 dwelling coverage).
e. Lenders use PITI as the baseline "all-in" monthly housing payment when calculating affordability and debt-to-income ratios.

HOUSING AFFORDABILITY IN KAZAKHSTAN

Housing affordability in Kazakhstan is relatively low, making it difficult for lower- and middle-income families, as well as young or first-time buyers, to purchase homes. The housing finance system is largely influenced by state-owned institutions and subsidy programs aimed at specific income and social groups. However, these programs often compete with, rather than support, commercial bank mortgage offerings. Only the highest-income groups typically have access to market-based and developer-partnered mortgage options. Government-subsidized loans through Otbasy Bank (OTB) are available to lower-income and vulnerable groups, and the National Bank of Kazakhstan's (NBK's) 7-20-25 program serves middle- to upper-income borrowers purchasing new homes. Table 3.1 presents key features of the main housing-finance products available to households in Kazakhstan.

In the absence of detailed portfolio-level data, the calculations in this chapter take all the products shown in table 3.1 with a weighted (by origination share) average loan size of T 15 million and average legal tenor of 180 months. The average OTB loan size is likely slightly lower, while the average size of mortgages from other second-tier banks is slightly higher. All products have a level-pay repayment structure and are issued in local currency. Note that OTB products marked in table 3.1 with "loan-to-value 100%" calculate monthly payments on the loan and deposit, not just the outstanding loan amount.

Based on the features of mortgage loan products shown in table 3.1, table 3.2 illustrates the household income needed to obtain loans with a prudent 50 percent gross payment-to-income (PTI) ratio.[2] This calculation uses a loan amount of T 15 million, which is the average as reported by lenders and OTB.

TABLE 3.1 Key housing finance options for Kazakhstani families

LENDER	SUBSIDY SOURCE	INTEREST RATE (PER YEAR, %)	NOTES
OTB @2% (LTV 100%)	Budget	2	S&L product with social eligibility
OTB @5% (LTV 50%)	Budget	5	S&L product with income or social eligibility
OTB @6% (LTV 100%)	Budget	6	Accelerated S&L product
Banks via NBK subsidy program @7%	Central bank	7	Subsidized mortgage for new construction
OTB @9% (LTV 100%)	Budget	9	Mainstream S&L product
Banks @15%	n.a.	~15	Developer-linked loans for new construction
Banks @20%	n.a.	~20	Common mortgage, no subsidy

Source: Original table for this publication.
Note: LTV = loan-to-value ratio; n.a. = not applicable; NBK = National Bank of Kazakhstan; OTB = Otbasy Bank; S&L = savings and loan.

TABLE 3.2 Required family income for prevailing housing finance options (stylized)

PRODUCT	INTEREST RATE (PER YEAR, %)	LOAN TERM (MONTHS)	MONTHLY PAYMENT ON LOAN OF T 15 MILLION (T)[a]	REQUIRED FAMILY INCOME FOR GROSS PTI OF 50% (T PER MONTH)
OTB @2% (LTV 100%)	2	180	193,000	386,000
OTB @5%	5	180	118,000	237,000
OTB @6% (LTV 100%)	6	180	253,000	506,000
NBK program @7%	7	180	135,000	270,000
OTB @9% (LTV 100%)	9	180	304,000	609,000
Banks @15%	15	180	210,000	420,000
Banks @20%	20	180	263,000	526,000

Source: Original table for this publication.
Note: LTV = loan-to-value ratio; NBK = National Bank of Kazakhstan; OTB = Otbasy Bank; PTI = payment-to-income ratio.
a. Calculated considering borrower income from deposit at OTB and rounded to the nearest 1,000.

Note that because the spatial distribution of provided housing finance is skewed heavily toward Almaty and Astana, the calculations in the table consider "actual" affordability, whereas calculating more "theoretical" affordability would use a lower loan amount, congruent with relative house prices by region.[3]

Interestingly, some OTB products may carry a higher effective LTV rate. The features of certain OTB products include using 100 percent LTV for payment calculation purposes, regardless of the borrower's actual down payment. For example, even though the nominal interest rate for the "OTB @2%" product listed in table 3.2 is 2 percent per year, the monthly payment for a loan of the same size would be higher than the "OTB @5%" mortgage, at least initially. In most OTB products, as detailed in table 3.3, the calculation uses actual LTV after some time.

Finally, table 3.3 combines data on incomes and mortgage products to estimate housing affordability by household income level. It overlays the monthly income distribution for an urban family of 3.1 persons (shown in the second column) with the per-product required income per month (shown across the rows) to indicate housing finance options that households at different income levels can prudently afford.

TABLE 3.3 Housing affordability, by product (stylized)

INCOME GROUP	FAMILY INCOME (T PER MONTH)	OTB @5%	NBK PROGRAM @7%	OTB @2% (LTV 100%)	BANKS @15%	OTB @6% (LTV 100%)	BANKS @20%	OTB @9% (LTV 100%)
Decile 1	127,000	n.a.	n.a.	n.a.	n.a.	n.a.	n.a.	n.a.
Decile 2	167,000	n.a.	n.a.	n.a.	n.a.	n.a.	n.a.	n.a.
Decile 3	192,000	n.a.	n.a.	n.a.	n.a.	n.a.	n.a.	n.a.
Decile 4	218,000	n.a.	n.a.	n.a.	n.a.	n.a.	n.a.	n.a.
Decile 5	246,000	237,000	n.a.	n.a.	n.a.	n.a.	n.a.	n.a.
Decile 6	283,000	237,000	270,000	n.a.	n.a.	n.a.	n.a.	n.a.
Decile 7	326,000	237,000	270,000	n.a.	n.a.	n.a.	n.a.	n.a.
Decile 8	386,000	237,000	270,000	386,000	n.a.	n.a.	n.a.	n.a.
Decile 9	484,000	237,000	270,000	386,000	420,000	n.a.	n.a.	n.a.
Decile 10	817,000	237,000	270,000	386,000	420,000	506,000	526,000	609,000
		Prevailing housing finance products and required family monthly income						

Source: Original table for this publication.
Note: LTV = loan-to-value ratio; NBK = National Bank of Kazakhstan; OTB = Otbasy Bank. The table shows affordability for an average urban family of 3.1 persons; the required income per decile is rounded to the nearest 10,000. LTV = loan-to-value ratio; n.a. = not applicable; NBK = National Bank of Kazakhstan; OTB = Otbasy Bank.

Families in deciles 1–4 are generally considered “low income”; those in deciles 5–8 are considered “middle income”; and those in deciles 9–10 are considered “high income.” It is reasonable to expect housing ownership subsidies to be targeted at middle-income families. High-income households should not expect any explicit subsidies, and families in lower-income deciles likely do not have the wherewithal to own a home and are expected to use rental or social (free or near-free) housing solutions.

Overall, untargeted OTB loans and market-priced mortgages from other second-tier banks (STBs)—which make up over 70 percent of 2024 originations (90,000+ loans)—are the least affordable products; they are available only to the top-two deciles (20 percent) of households by income. This dynamic illustrates that much of the mortgage demand is concentrated in the better-off segments of the population, notwithstanding the number of significantly subsidized mortgage products.

AFFORDABILITY SENSITIVITY OVERVIEW

It is clear that housing affordability largely depends on the monthly mortgage payment, which, in turn, is determined by the loan amount and the annual interest rate. Because this report focuses on housing finance (rather than real estate supply or household income-earning opportunities), it examines potential financial policy or mortgage-market measures that can materially affect affordability. There are broadly two such measures: (1) mortgage product design and (2) prevailing interest rate. Real estate supply, prices, and household income are assumed as given (exogenous) in the near term—although this assumption will not hold in the medium to long term.[4]

Based on the previous discussion, ordinary mortgages from STBs appear to have relatively prudent underwriting and down-payment requirements. Mortgages from OTB benefit from an intrinsically lower interest rate, although somewhat convoluted loan mechanics significantly increase monthly payments (at least for initial periods).

One reasonable affordability lever to examine is, therefore, the mortgage interest rate, assuming that other variables remain unchanged in the near term. As the annual mortgage interest rate, ceteris paribus, determines the amount of the monthly loan repayment, projecting the affordability impact of interest rate dynamics may be illuminating for market stakeholders.

Figure 3.1 illustrates the stepwise impact of interest rate changes on housing finance affordability. A meaningful decrease (2–4 percent) in prevailing mortgage rates apparently is needed to nudge affordability up toward the next income decile. This finding may provide insights for the regulator, in particular. A downward rate movement—if supported by monetary policy actions—is unlikely to be immediately reflected in increased housing affordability, as evidenced by the rise in mortgage demand.

FIGURE 3.1

Impact of changes in mortgage interest rates on affordability

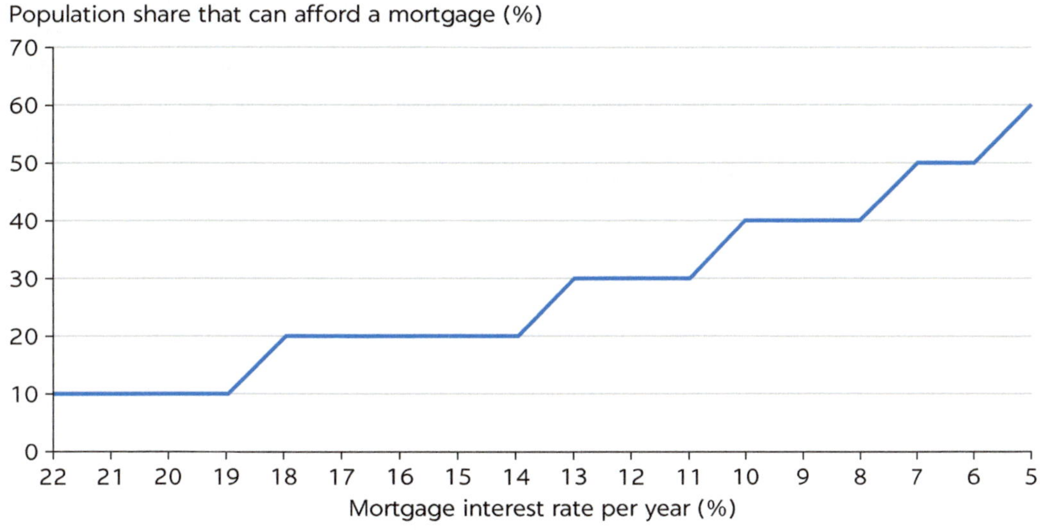

Source: Original figure for this report using World Bank calculations.

Note: Assumptions used for the purposes of this calculation are the same as for the affordability calculations used earlier: loan amount, T 15 million; loan term, 180 months; 50 percent gross payment-to-income ratio. As the rates decrease along the *x*-axis, the affordability curve plotted on the *y*-axis indicates an increase in the share of the population that can afford a typical mortgage. The figure shows a simple, static, single-factor analysis, that is, income distribution and property price characteristics are assumed unchanged. This is unrealistic, as both will likely exhibit evolutions in the context of reduction in interest rates. Thus, the analysis should be regarded as a rough illustration of affordability sensitivity to interest rates and a "what-if-the-rates-had-been-lower" scenario. Although monetary policy signals are available to both the financial sector and construction industry, there is still a natural supply-side permit-to-completion lag (due to the physical construction cycle and administrative procedures). This delay may reduce affordability in the immediate term via increased prices.

NOTES

1. Many definitions of *housing affordability* exist, and all link family incomes, prevailing housing finance solutions, and real estate prices. Some of the common ones are household focused and compare average incomes to average house prices in various ways. Methodologically, it is important to rigorously use median (not average) house prices and a proper national income distribution.
2. The *PTI ratio* is the ratio of monthly mortgage payment to borrower income before mandatory expenses like taxes and other living expenses (such as payments for sustenance or for other debts).
3. While the 2024 average national price per square meter of a newly constructed urban dwelling is about T 395,000, the average for Almaty and Astana is T 589,000, or about 50 percent higher. Thus, it may be reasonable to assume that a similar dwelling by size and other characteristics would carry a congruently lower price outside of those two regions. See KHC, https://homeportal.kz/ru/useful-information-details/92.
4. Especially in the context of uncertain supply elasticity and monetary policy easing—that is, in case of rapid interest rate decline—the supply of residential real estate will likely not catch up to the increased demand, and thus prices may increase.

REFERENCES

Bankrate. 2025. "Property Tax Rates by State: What to Expect in Your Area." May 7, 2025. https://www.bankrate.com/real-estate/property-tax-by-state/.

Kazakhstan Housing Company. n.d. "Analytics: Useful Information Page List." https://homeportal.kz/ru/useful-information-details/92.

National Statistical Bureau, Agency for Strategic Planning and Reforms. 2025. "The Main Indicators of Income Differentiation of Population of the Republic of Kazakhstan (II Quarter of 2025)." October 31, 2025. https://stat.gov.kz/en/industries/labor-and-income/stat-life/publications/448101/.

4 Otbasy Bank and Its Role in the Market

BACKGROUND AND KEY FINANCIAL INDICATORS

Otbasy Bank (OTB) is a national housing finance development institution that operates a savings and loan (S&L) system and implements public subsidy programs. OTB was established in 2003 and in 2013 became a subsidiary of Baiterek Holding. It is a second-tier bank (STB) regulated and supervised by the Agency of the Republic of Kazakhstan for Regulation and Development of Financial Market and is a member of the deposit insurance system. In 2024, the housing legislation was amended to grant OTB the status of a national development institution responsible for implementing state support measures to improve housing conditions. This legislation transfers functions from local executive bodies to OTB, which is now responsible for distributing housing to socially vulnerable groups and managing the respective database.

By the end of 2024, OTB reported assets of T 4.28 trillion (US$8.4 billion), making it the fourth-largest bank in Kazakhstan by asset size. It recorded net income of T 121 billion (US$236 million), with a return on average equity of 19 percent and a cost-to-income ratio of 17.4 percent, indicating a high level of operational efficiency. In May 2025, the OTB Board of Directors (BoD) approved distribution of 70 percent of 2024 net income as dividends to be paid in 2025; the amount was just under T 85 billion (US$165 million). The bank's cost of risk (net provisions charge over average gross portfolio) is also low—well below 0.5 percent per year. By end-2024, its loan portfolio exceeded T 3 trillion (US$5.9 billion), with annual loan disbursements surpassing T 1 trillion. Holding more than 50 percent of the total mortgage market portfolio in Kazakhstan, it is the largest player in the mortgage segment by volume.

The key strategic directions for OTB in 2024–33 are discussed in box 4.1.

Box 4.1

Key strategic directions for Otbasy Bank, 2024–33

Otbasy Bank (OTB) has adopted a strategy to strengthen its role as both a key social policy institution and a commercially competitive bank. Approved by the Board of Directors on February 27, 2024, the strategy aligns with the overarching goals of its shareholder, the National Managing Holding "Baiterek." OTB seeks market leadership in long-term savings and mortgage lending, while building its reputation as the best employer in the domestic banking sector.

The bank describes its mission as "strengthening the sense of Homeland by ensuring families have their own housing and improving long-term well-being" (Otbasy Bank 2023b)

OTB' s strategic focus areas include the following:

- *Social partnership with the state.* OTB is the sole financial institution responsible for implementing government housing support programs in Kazakhstan.
- *Enhancement of services.* The bank plans to enhance its client services, expand product offerings, and modernize information technology systems to compete effectively in the financial market.
- *Bank sustainability.* The focus on balanced risk management, financial stability, and a performance-driven human resources system supports long-term growth.
- *Environmental, social, governance (ESG) integration.* Implementation of ESG principles across operations supports responsible and sustainable banking.

BUSINESS MODEL

OTB operations are financed primarily through customer deposits. By the end of 2024, these accounted for approximately 75 percent of total liabilities (T 3.6 trillion, equal to US$7 billion), resulting in a loan-to-deposit ratio of around 127 percent. Wholesale funding accounted for just over 15 percent of total liabilities, with 44 percent of the wholesale funding provided as loans from the Ministry of Finance, 25 percent from the Asian Development Bank, 24 percent from other multilateral lenders, and the remainder from Baiterek Holdings.

OTB operates a national voluntary S&L system (Ministry of Justice, Institute of Legislation and Legal Information 2000), which encourages households to accumulate dedicated savings over a specified period at lower interest rates than those available on the open market. In exchange, households become eligible for lower-interest mortgage loans.

The OTB S&L down-payment subsidy works as follows: A depositor receives an annual budgetary premium equal to 20 percent of monies deposited that year up to the limit of 200 times the monthly calculation amount (MCA), which is an annually revised number used as a basis for calculating fines, taxes, and the like. The 2025 MCA was set to T 3,932, so the maximum annual premium per depositor in 2025 was 200 × T 3,932 × 20 percent, or T 157,280. Thus, an individual needs to deposit at least T 786,400 to receive the maximum possible premium.

Apart from subsidies on clients' deposits, there are also OTB bond coupon subsidies. These bonds are issued at market rate, but interest payments above 7 percent per year are subsidized, as OTB is compensated by the Government of Kazakhstan (Ministry of Construction) in the amount equal to the difference between 7 percent and the actual coupon rate of its bonds outstanding. These could add as much as one-third to the volume of subsidies on clients' deposits (according to 2025 estimations). The flow of subsidies is depicted in figure 4.1. and evolution over time presented in table 4.1.

Box 4.2 discusses the implications of the 2026 government budget freeze for OTB's client deposit premium subsidies.

FIGURE 4.1

Flow of Otbasy Bank dividends, client deposit premiums, and subsidies for the bank's bond interest payments above 7 percent

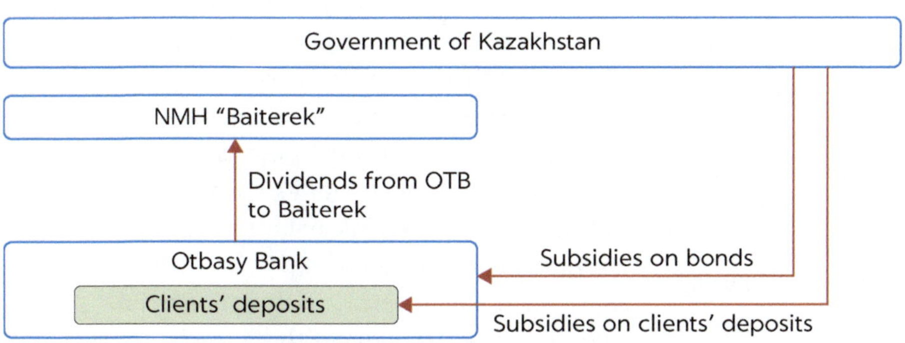

Sources: Original figure for this publication using data from National Managing Holding and Otbasy Bank (2024, n.d.b).

TABLE 4.1 Volume of Otbasy Bank dividends and state deposit premiums, 2020–24 (T, billions)

FUNDS FLOW	2020	2021	2022	2023	2024	2020–24 TOTAL
Dividends from Otbasy Bank to Baiterek	8.3	Not paid	32.9	67.2	44.3	152.7
State subsidies on clients' deposits	50.5	60.6	75.1	81.9	92.8	360.9

Sources: National Bank of Kazakhstan (2026) and Otbasy Bank (2021, 2024a, 2024b, n.d.a, n.d.b).

Box 4.2

Implications of the 2026 budget freeze for Otbasy Bank's state deposit premiums

In October 2025, several Kazakhstani media outlets—citing officials from the government and the Mazhilis (Parliament) of the Republic of Kazakhstan—reported that the expenditure side of the 2026 state budget allocated no funds to pay state premiums on deposit top-ups made by Otbasy Bank (OTB) to depositors in 2025 (InBusiness.kz 2025; Kursiv Media 2025).

The 2025 premiums could be paid from OTB's own resources. According to these reports, the bank's net profit for 2024 was approximately T 120 billion, while the amount required to pay the 2025 deposit premiums was approximately T 90 billion. Media reports did not include confirmation of this information by OTB, and there was no information on whether the state budget for 2027 and subsequent years would provide funds to pay OTB depositor premiums.

This is a material development. The state premiums on OTB deposit contributions are a key element of the savings and loan (S&L) model, and their absence could significantly affect affordability for OTB borrowers and negatively impact the bank's financial model and performance. Such significant changes need to be managed with delicacy toward over 3 million OTB depositors. Moreover, the subsidies' broad implications for social and housing finance policy need to be considered. OTB depositors are not at present affected, as at least in 2025, the bank's own resources seem sufficient to substitute the funds from the budget.

Paying depositor premiums from OTB's own funds could negatively affect the bank's financial metrics, reducing its capital adequacy ratio, potentially constraining asset growth, and consequently limiting mortgage issuance to households. A permanent decision to finance depositor premiums from the bank's own resources would require OTB to revisit its strategy and financial model, specifically regarding financial indicators and demand forecasting for prospective borrowers. It would be challenging, for example, to maintain a fixed premium amount per depositor given uncertain financial results for the bank year by year. A permanent change of the premium contribution mechanism is also likely to have material accounting implications for the bank.

By the end of 2025, it was unclear whether the change represented a temporary freezing or a more permanent approach toward budgetary allocation of funds for S&L deposit premiums. However, if this change is a permanent one, it could negatively affect the efficiency and effectiveness of housing policy pursued through OTB as the single operator of state programs. In addition, it would be reasonable to suggest that expansion of the S&L model to other second-tier banks might not be attractive to commercial banks in Kazakhstan under these conditions and, thus, related recent legal initiatives might not be relevant.

While OTB is intended to act as a tool for affordable housing via long-term savings and access to preferential mortgage rates, its practical effectiveness is not uniform across different segments of the population. The system predominantly benefits individuals who already possess sufficient financial stability to accumulate the required initial savings within the minimum savings period. For this group, participation is economically rational: The combined benefits of state premiums on deposits and preferential loan terms on mortgage loans often offsets real estate price increases (inflation) during the savings period. As a result, such participants can leverage the program to mitigate rising housing costs, thereby making homeownership more accessible to them.

For the broader population, particularly those without significant initial capital, the program structure has some limitations. Although participants eventually gain access to below-market mortgage rates, the deposit rates offered by the bank are low, yielding returns that fail to keep pace with the rapid nominal growth in housing prices. As a result, while individuals are required to save a specific initial down payment to qualify, the real value of their accumulated savings weakens relative to housing market dynamics. By the time loan eligibility is achieved, property prices may have increased to the point that even the preferential mortgage conditions do not allow participants to take out a mortgage. Thus, the program's effectiveness is diminished not only by participants' limited disposable income but also by the inherent opportunity costs associated with tying up capital in low-yield deposits.

Table 4.2 illustrates select global institutional modalities for S&L systems, highlighting how similar models have been structured, governed, and funded across advanced and emerging economies. These examples are particularly relevant for OTB, as they provide concrete benchmarks for assessing alternative design choices around funding mechanisms, pricing structures, risk allocation, and governance—especially in systems where S&L institutions play a systemically important role in housing finance. The cross-country cases underscore that, while S&L models can effectively channel long-term household savings into mortgage lending, their impact on affordability and market development depends critically on institutional safeguards, competitive neutrality, and integration with broader financial and capital markets.

Table 4.3 illustrates key S&L system strengths and risks and their likely applicability to OTB S&L implementation.

TABLE 4.2 Select global examples of savings and loan modalities

MODALITY	EXAMPLE	DESCRIPTION
Mutual building society	**United Kingdom: Building societies**	Building societies involve member and depositor ownership, with a focus on retail savings and mortgage lending. The model is originate-to-hold, and profits are returned to members through lower rates and bonuses. As of 2024, mortgage balances were ~£397 billion, or 24 percent of all UK mortgage balances. Gross lending was ~£36 billion.
Contractual S&L system (Bausparen)	**Germany: Bausparkassen** **Austria: Bausparkassen/ Wüstenrot**	Within these are specialized building and loan associations, customers sign a "saving + loan" contract (save, qualify, then receive a preferential fixed loan). There is a large stock of pre-priced loan contracts; funding is via customer deposits; and these are strongly regulated. The aggregate portfolio for all Bausparkassen is ~€930 billion (including savings and contract sums). The Wüstenrot Group's total assets are ~€72 billion.

continued

TABLE 4.2 Select global examples of savings and loan modalities *(continued)*

MODALITY	EXAMPLE	DESCRIPTION
Voluntary social housing fund	**Brazil: Brazilian Savings and Loan System (SBPE)**	This contractual S&L system is funded by mandated or incentivized retail savings (cadernetas de poupança) earmarked for housing lending at regulated rates. It operates alongside other pillars (FGTS, SFH, and SFI) and channels retail savings into mortgage finance. Caixa Econômica Federal (public) is the dominant SBPE originator; private banks also lend using SBPE resources. SBPE annual mortgage originations in 2024 were ~US$30 billion, or half of the national total. Retail savings were ~US$71 billion.
Compulsory social housing fund	**Mexico: INFONAVIT**	This mandatory S&L system is funded by formal sector employers' contributions, which can be used as collateral or for down payment on a housing loan. The total credit portfolio is ~US$88 billion, which include tens of millions of worker accounts. Approximately 75 percent of loans go to lower- and middle-income formal sector workers. The 2024 outstanding portfolio is ~US$85 billion, with ~US$13 billion in originations and 40 percent of the total market.

Sources: For the UK building societies: Building Societies Association (2024). For the German and Austrian Bausparkassen: Bausparkassen, "Bausparen in Germany," https://www.bausparkassen.de/presse/daten-fakten/, Wüstenrot/W&W 2024. For the Brazilian S&L system: Banco Central do Brasil, "Savings and Loans Associations," https://www.bcb.gov.br/en/financialstability/savings_loans_associations; Caixa Econômica Federal, "Crédito Imobiliário CAIXA," https://www.caixa.gov.br/voce/habitacao/Paginas/default.aspx. For Mexico's INFONAVIT: INFONAVIT (2024) and; Fitch Ratings (2024).
Note: FGTS = Fundo de Garantia do Tempo de Serviço (Severance Indemnity Fund); S&L = savings and loan; SFH = Sistema Financeiro da Habitação (Housing Finance System); SFI = Sistema de Financiamento Imobiliário (Real Estate Financing System); SPBE = Brazilian Savings and Loan System; UK = United Kingdom; US = United States.

TABLE 4.3 Typical savings and loan strengths and challenges and applicability to Otbasy Bank

STRENGTHS (RELATIVE TO THE MARKET)	APPLICABLE TO OTB?
Member-centric ethos. Many S&Ls are mutuals whose profits are recycled to offer lower mortgage rates or higher savings returns.	No, OTB is an SOE
Natural countercyclical instrument. The more limited responsiveness of funding cost to monetary policy makes S&Ls attractive during high-interest-rate cycles.	Yes
Local presence and relationships. S&Ls have a strong community focus; underwriting is based on local knowledge, personal service, and flexible assessment.	Yes, in the context of targeted subsidy programs
Long-term fixed-rate loans. S&Ls are willing to fund 15–30-year fixed-rate mortgages.	No, other STBs offer loans at similar terms
Lower barriers for first-time buyers. S&Ls offer conservative lending, sometimes with programs or favorable LTVs for first-time borrowers.	Yes, in the context of targeted subsidy programs
Aligned incentives. S&Ls' retention of loans on the balance sheet creates incentives to work with borrowers through repayment difficulties.	Yes
Perceived stability and trust. S&Ls are seen as safe, conservative institutions—attractive for borrowers wary of large universal banks.	Yes, to some extent due to state ownership of OTB

continued

TABLE 4.3 Typical savings and loan strengths and challenges and applicability to Otbasy Bank *(continued)*

STRENGTHS (RELATIVE TO THE MARKET)	APPLICABLE TO OTB?
Natural target market segmentation. S&Ls are particularly attractive to first-time homeowners, young families, and lower- and middle-income families.	Yes, in the context of targeted subsidy programs
Challenges	
Liquidity runs. Concentration in retail deposits can become a vulnerability if depositors flee.	Yes, to some extent
Credit and market risk. A concentrated loan portfolio means a housing downturn or borrower stress quickly impact capital.	Yes, to some extent
Concentration and operational risk. S&Ls' small scale, legacy systems, or limited diversification can amplify shocks.	No
Structural volume limits. Pure deposit-based funding leads to hard limits on origination; a sophisticated financial model is needed to align deposit funding with origination volumes, likely via credit rationing.	Yes, although OTB issues debt to avoid limitations of deposit-only funding
Potential subsidy capture. Where many small depositors (likely lower income) fund few borrowers (likely higher income), subsidy capture is possible.	Yes[a]
Subsidy risk. S&Ls' appeal depends largely on public support for deposits; reductions in subsidy may discourage new members and negatively affect institutional stability and origination capacity.	Yes

Source: Original table for this publication.
Note: LTV = loan-to-value ratio; OTB = Otbasy Bank; S&L = savings and loan; SOE = state-owned enterprise; STB = second-tier bank.
a. For example, OTB has 3,548,114 current deposits and only 642,087 loans issued. https://hcsbk.kz/en/.

OTBASY BANK PRODUCTS AND TARGETING

OTB offers both targeted housing solutions for borrowers meeting specific eligibility requirements, in the context of operating numerous government programs, and untargeted solutions, which can be accessed by all depositors after a specified savings period. As discussed in the section "Housing Affordability in Kazakhstan" in chapter 3, untargeted OTB solutions are accessible to borrowers in the top income decile and directly compete with mortgages from other STBs for potential clients. About one-third of OTB originations are targeted at borrowers with lower incomes and socioeconomic characteristics. Notably, all depositors at OTB receive a government down-payment subsidy (deposit premium), regardless of which loan solution they obtain.

OTB is responsible for implementing a range of state housing initiatives. Acting as a financial agent for the government, the bank allocates public funds and otherwise collaborates with government authorities, municipalities, and public sector employers to implement housing policies (provide concessional lending) for target population segments. These include young families, low-income households, rural residents, military personnel, large families, orphans, individuals with disabilities, early-career researchers, and civil servants.
In addition to its role in saving and lending, the bank also operates nonlending programs, including the allocation of rental housing to vulnerable populations.

Given this context, it would be appropriate to introduce a standard mortgage insurance modality that provides first-loss partial credit risk coverage. Thus, a relatively small (15–25 percent) coverage essentially supplements the borrower's down payment for underwriting and prudential ratio purposes; it also allows families without a large down payment to obtain a loan without higher perceived risks and, thus, at the market-average interest rate. From a lender's perspective, this solution reduces capital consumption (subject to strict policy terms and conditions), as the insured portion of the loan may be included by the regulator in calculating the loan-to-value (LTV) ratio.

OTB provides a range of savings and mortgage solutions, including preliminary housing loans (interim financing) and standard mortgage loans for clients who have completed the savings phase. Mortgage rates under these programs are generally below market averages, reflecting OTB's access to low-cost funding through customer deposits, as well as the government's bonuses on savings deposits. By the end of 2024, preliminary and intermediate loans each comprised about 35 percent of OTB's portfolio.[1] The rest were housing loans. The types of loans are described as follows:

- *Preliminary loans* are typically linked to specific government and regional programs, such as Svoy Dom, Umai, and Zhana Baspana. These loans are designed for borrowers at an earlier savings stage, with contributions ranging from 10 percent to 50 percent of the required amount. Interest rates vary significantly depending on the borrower's category and savings, ranging from 2 percent to 14.4 percent per year. Savings contributions continue throughout the preliminary loan period. Once the savings target is reached, a housing loan is issued to repay the outstanding balance on the preliminary loan. Terms for these loans typically range from 6 months to 10 years.
- *Intermediate loans* provide borrowers with access to financing before they fully complete the savings cycle. These loans are available to those who have saved or contributed at least 50 percent of the required amount and achieved a valuation score of 5. Interest rates range from 2 percent to 8.5 percent per year, with repayment terms of up to 25 years. While these loans enable borrowers to acquire housing more quickly, clients are required to continue saving to eventually transition to a lower-interest-rate housing loan. Until then, interest is charged on the full loan amount (100 percent of the outstanding principal, effective LTV of 100 percent). Once the borrower transitions to the housing loan, the accumulated savings, which represent at least 50 percent of the property value, are used to partially repay the loan principal, effectively reducing the outstanding debt by half.
- *Housing loans* represent the final and most favorable stage within the system. They are available to depositors who have accumulated at least 50 percent of the required amount over a period from 3 years (the mandatory minimum)

to 15 years. Interest rates range from 3.5 percent to 5 percent per year. However, for certain socially vulnerable groups, such as participants in the Bakytty Otbasy program, the rate is fixed at 2 percent per year. Loan terms vary from 6 months to 25 years. To qualify, borrowers must meet several criteria: reach the required savings threshold, achieve a specified valuation score, provide collateral, and demonstrate solvency.

OTB also offers green mortgages for the purchase or refurbishment of newly constructed properties certified according to local or international energy efficiency standards.[2] Green mortgages offer specific privileges on interest rates or other mortgage terms; as of early November 2025, 13 eligible real estate developments were available, primarily in Astana.

Table 4.4 details key housing programs offered by OTB, each aimed at expanding access to affordable housing for different citizen categories in Kazakhstan through a combination of savings schemes and preferential mortgage terms.

OTBASY BANK'S CORPORATE GOVERNANCE CONSIDERATIONS

OTB operates under a governance framework intended to align its housing finance mandate with Kazakhstan's socioeconomic objectives; however, this framework limits operational autonomy and exposes the bank to political interference.[3] Strengthening OTB's corporate governance in line with the Organisation for Economic Co-operation and Development (OECD) guidelines and the Basel framework is, therefore, critical to reinforce operational autonomy, effective risk management, and the bank's long-term sustainability. Currently, the independence and effectiveness of both the BoD and Management Board are constrained, as the chief executive officer is appointed exclusively by the sole shareholder, contrary to the *OECD Guidelines on Corporate Governance of State-Owned Enterprises 2024* (OECD 2024), which assign this authority to the board. Without this mandate, the board cannot fully exercise oversight or be held accountable for performance. In addition, the bank's charter allows the sole shareholder to issue direct operational instructions and override board or management decisions, further conflicting with OECD principles on operational autonomy and increasing the risk of undue political influence. Box 4.3 presents more detailed considerations.

TABLE 4.4 Key public support programs channeled through Otbasy Bank

PROGRAM	DESCRIPTION
Development of Housing and Public Utilities Infrastructure for 2023–29	Targets borrowers seeking affordable new housing and offers mortgage rates of up to 5 percent per year with lower down-payment requirements; the goal is to support affordable homeownership through concessional mortgage terms and structured savings mechanisms. Loans are provided at rates of up to 5 percent per year. The minimum down payment is 10 percent. Housing is offered at preferential prices, primarily for newly constructed properties.
Bakytty Otbasy (2-10-20)	Supports socially vulnerable groups, including large families, orphans, persons with disabilities, and families raising children with disabilities. Eligible properties are restricted to municipally allocated housing. The loan interest rate is 2 percent per year. The down payment is at least 10 percent, and the loan term is up to 20 years. Participants may purchase housing only in the region where they are registered on the official housing waiting list maintained by local authorities.
Svoy Dom	Is available to OTB depositors with at least T 500,000 (~US$975). Interest rates are initially 6–7 percent per year and may be reduced over time to 3.5–5 percent per year. The down payment is at least 20 percent. The maximum loan amount is T 100 million (~US$195,000), with a loan term of up to 25 years.
Zhana Baspana	Provides affordable mortgages for recipients of state housing payments (certain citizen categories, such as military, employees of special state bodies, and law enforcement agencies, as well as low-income families and tenants of the state housing stock). Down payment is at least 15 percent. Interest rates range from 3.5 percent to 5 percent per year.
Rental Subsidy Program	Is for lower-income families, where the average monthly family income over the past 6 months does not exceed 1 minimum subsistence level per family member. Applicants must provide proof of registration as in need of housing in accordance with the Law of the Republic of Kazakhstan, "On Housing Relations," and must belong to one of the eligible categories for state support, including persons with disabilities, families raising children with disabilities, orphans, and others.
OTB Housing Program for Young Scientists (2023–27)	Offers housing loans to young researchers working at research institutes and universities in Kazakhstan who are officially registered as needing housing. The down payment is 10–50 percent, and the interest rate is 5 percent per year. Loan terms are up to 25 years, with preliminary loans available for periods ranging from 6 months to 8 years. Once 50 percent of the savings target has been achieved, the interest rate may be reduced to 3.5–5 percent per year. The maximum loan amount is T 20 million (~US$39,000).
Zhas Otbasy Program	Is designed to support newly married couples. One or both spouses must open a new deposit account and maintain savings for at least 1 year. The loan is provided at a fixed interest rate of 6 percent per year for a term of 6–9 years, with a maximum loan amount of T 100 million (~US$195,000). At the time of the loan application, the borrower must have accumulated at least 50 percent of the property's purchase price or be able to contribute it to the deposit.

Sources: World Bank Group compilations based on publicly available program documents.
Note: OTB = Otbasy Bank.

Box 4.3

Summary of Otbasy Bank's corporate governance review

Otbasy Bank (OTB), wholly owned by the National Managing Holding "Baiterek," is governed by a sole shareholder, a board of directors (BoD), a management board (MB), and a system of board and management committees. This structure is intended to align the bank's activities with Kazakhstan's broader socioeconomic and housing policy objectives.

Board of Directors and Management Board

The current BoD arrangements only partially reflect good international practice. The BoD is chaired by the representative of the sole shareholder rather than an independent director and consists of five members: the shareholder representative, the chief executive officer (CEO), and three independent directors. Independent directors have relevant expertise, but there is no staggered board structure, and all three are already in their second or third 3-year terms, limiting board refreshment and continuity planning.

CEO appointment and dismissal are reserved for the sole shareholder. By contrast, the Organisation for Economic Co-operation and Development guidelines assign this function to the board. Without such authority, the BoD's ability to exercise effective oversight of management and be held accountable for the bank's performance is constrained. Furthermore, OTB's charter allows the sole shareholder to issue binding operational instructions and to overturn internal decisions of the BoD and MB, an arrangement that undermines operational autonomy and increases the risk of undue political interference.

OTB has four specialized BoD committees. While the CEO is appropriately not a member of any of these, the BoD chair sits on all four committees. In two cases, the composition largely mirrors that of the full board. This concentration increases the chair's dominance and weakens the value added by committees. The Audit Committee's mandate also extends to considering financing and credit decisions, a responsibility that is not in line with the Basel framework and that can create conflicts of interest. Risk governance deviates from Basel recommendations, as the chair of the Risk and Internal Controls Committee simultaneously chairs the Strategy and Corporate Development Committee.

Control Environment and Risk Management

The internal control system is based on the "three lines" model, an internationally accepted model for internal controls and risk management—the "three lines of defence" model—developed and guided by the Committee of Sponsoring Organizations of the Treadway Commission. However, there is no clear evidence that the Internal Audit Department's regulations align with the latest Global Internal Audit Standards.

Risk management meets national regulatory requirements but diverges from Basel good practice. The chief risk officer (CRO) is also deputy chair of the MB and chairs several management committees, including the key Credit Committee. Basel guidance discourages CRO involvement in revenue-generating decisions and credit approvals to avoid conflicts and preserve the risk function's independence. A more appropriate model would limit the CRO to a veto or challenge role.

The compliance function appears broadly aligned with regulatory expectations. However, disclosure does not clearly indicate when and by whom the set of anti-corruption standards were approved.

Environmental, social, and governance (ESG) considerations, including environmental and social risks, are integrated into OTB's 2024–33

continued

Box 4.3, Summary of Otbasy Bank's corporate governance review *(continued)*

strategy. A dedicated Sustainable Development Strategy approved in 2025 includes ESG key performance indicators. The bank's Risk Management Policy also explicitly includes ESG aspects. Sustainability oversight has been assigned to the Strategy and Corporate Development Committee, and OTB has received an ESG rating of 3 from Sustainable Fitch (2025).

Disclosure and Transparency

OTB prepares International Financial Reporting Standards financial statements audited under the International Standards on Auditing and discloses information on state support and subsidies. PwC has been the external auditor for 11 years; the bank has an auditor interaction policy, including audit partner rotation, but the long-standing relationship may affect the auditor's perceived independence.

The timeliness of reporting lags behind good international practice. As of July 2025, the latest publicly available annual and sustainability reports are for 2023, whereas the leading practice is to publish within 6 months of the year-end. Annual reports do not make the Dividend Policy publicly available. The sustainability report follows the Global Reporting Initiative and the Sustainability Accounting Standards Board (mortgage finance) standards.

Sources: OTB (2023a); OTB Audit Committee Regulation, https://hcsbk.kz/en/about-the-bank/corp-documents/; OTB Charter; and OTB reporting in English, https://hcsbk.kz/about-the-bank/reporting/go-2024/en/.

NOTES

1. The calculated return on the loan portfolio for 2024 is approximately 7.2 percent, reflecting the ratio of interest income generated from lending activities to the average loan portfolio over the period.
2. Otbasy Bank, "Зеленая ипотека," https://hcsbk.kz/ru/zelenaya-ipoteka/.
3. The corporate governance review is based on the publicly available information from the Otbasy Bank (OTB) corporate website at https://hcsbk.kz/, including the 2023 OTB annual report (https://hcsbk.kz/en/about-the-bank/reporting/); the Kazakhstani Stock Exchange (https://kase.kz/ru/listing/issuers/JSBN); and the Kazakhstani Depository of Financial Statements (https://opi.dfo.kz/ru/opi/list/278746062405000000/view). To the extent possible, the report has applied the methodologies of the World Bank Group, such as the Integrated State-Owned Enterprises Framework and the International Finance Corporation's Progression Matrixes for Financial Institutions and State-Owned Enterprises, with reference to good international practice and standards, including the Organisation for Economic Co-operation and Development's *Guidelines on Corporate Governance of State-Owned Enterprises 2024* (https://doi.org/10.1787/18a24f43-en) and the Basel Committee on Banking Supervision standards (https://www.bis.org/basel_framework/). The results of the corporate governance review must be treated with caution due to the scope limitations—that is, they are based only on a desk review of the publicly available information, which is affected by the timeliness of the data disclosed by the OTB (for example, OTB's 2024 annual report was not publicly available at the time of review), as well as by the data's completeness and accuracy. A full-scope analysis of the OTB's corporate governance practices should be undertaken to ensure that recommendations are complete, accurate, and based on the effectiveness of actual practices.

REFERENCES

Building Societies Association. 2024. "Building Societies Trading Update November 2024." November 28, 2024. https://www.bsa.org.uk/statistics/sector-info-performance/building-society-trading-updates/building-societies-trading-update-november-2024.

Fitch Ratings. 2024. "Fitch Affirms Infonavit's IDRs at 'BBB-'/'F3'; Outlook Stable." June 14, 2024. https://www.fitchratings.com/research/non-bank-financial-institutions/fitch-affirms-infonavit-idrs-at-bbb-f3-outlook-stable-14-06-2024.

InBusiness.kz. 2025. "The State Budget Did Not Allocate Funds for Bonuses for Otbasy Bank Clients." https://inbusiness.kz/index.php/ru/last/dengi-na-premii-klientam-otbasy-banka-ne-predusmotreli-v-gosbyudzhete.

INFONAVIT. 2024. "Informe Anual de Actividades 2024." https://portalmx.infonavit.org.mx/wps/wcm/connect/eac8add8-7c6b-4c7b-ae16-53228bb3f25f/Informe%2BAnual%2Bde%2BActividades%2B2024.pdf?CVID=pq8xONN&MOD=AJPERES.

Kursiv Media. 2025. "The State Bonus for Deposits at Otbasy Bank Will Not Be Paid from the Budget." https://kz.kursiv.media/2025-10-22/svan-kto-budet-platit-gospremiyu-po-vkladam-v-otbasy-banke-rasskazali-v-minfine/.

Ministry of Justice, Institute of Legislation and Legal Information. 2000. "On Housing Construction Savings in the Republic of Kazakhstan." Law of the Republic of Kazakhstan, December 7, 2000, No. 110. https://adilet.zan.kz/eng/docs/Z000000110_.

NAR (National Association of Realtors). 2025. "Buyers Reemerge: Lower Mortgage Rates Lift Fall Home Sales." November 20, 2025. *REALTOR® Magazine*. https://www.nar.realtor/magazine/real-estate-news/economy/buyers-reemerge-lower-mortgage-rates-lift-fall-home-sale.

National Bank of Kazakhstan. 2026. "Loans to the Economy from Second-Tier Banks (historical data)." https://nationalbank.kz/ru/news/loans-to-economy-from-second-tier-banks/rubrics/1840.

OECD (Organisation for Economic Co-operation and Development). 2024. *OECD Guidelines on Corporate Governance of State-Owned Enterprises 2024*. OECD Publishing. https://doi.org/10.1787/18a24f43-en.

Otbasy Bank. 2021. "More Than 50 Billion Tenge in State Bonuses Have Been Credited to the Accounts of Otbasy Bank Clients." https://hcsbk.kz/ru/news/archive-bank-news/bolee-50-mlrd-tenge-gosudarstvennoy-premii-zachisleno-na-scheta-klientov-otbasy-banka1.

Otbasy Bank. 2023a. *Annual Report 2023*. https://hcsbk.kz/en/about-the-bank/reporting/.

Otbasy Bank. 2023b. *Development Strategy*. https://hcsbk.kz/ru/about-the-bank/strategy/.

Otbasy Bank. 2024a. "Key Events of the Reporting Year." https://hcsbk.kz/about-the-bank/reporting/go-2024/en/klyucheve-sobtiya-otchetnogo-goda.html.

Otbasy Bank. 2024b. "Key Sustainability Events in 2024." https://hcsbk.kz/about-the-bank/reporting/our-2024/en/klyucheve-sobtiya-v-oblasti-ustochivogo-razvitiya-v-2024-godu.html.

Otbasy Bank. n.d.a. "Annual Reports." https://hcsbk.kz/en/about-the-bank/reporting/.

Otbasy Bank. n.d.b. "Information for Shareholders." https://hcsbk.kz/en/about-the-bank/information-for-shareholders/.

Sustainable Fitch. 2025. "Sustainable Fitch Affirms Otbasy's Entity Rating at '3.'" November 12, 2025. https://www.sustainablefitch.com/banks/sustainable-fitch-affirms-otbasys-entity-rating-at-3-12-11-2025.

Wüstenrot/W&W. 2024. *Annual Report 2024*. https://www.ww-ag.com/media/files_1/investor_relations_2/reports/annual_reports/2024_4/WuW_Annual_Report_2024.pdf.

5 Capital Market Solutions for Housing Finance

CONTEXT AND CURRENT STATE

The interrelation between the mortgage and capital markets in Kazakhstan is not obvious. While Otbasy Bank (OTB) and the Kazakhstan Housing Company (KHC) periodically tap the capital markets by issuing bonds, these issuances are largely not market based and are not directly linked to housing finance assets. The residential mortgage-backed securities (RMBS) market is currently not functioning, notwithstanding a generally well-developed capital market in terms of enabling environment, instruments, and infrastructure (Bango and Yoon 2024). In the corporate bond market—the area directly relevant for mortgage-related capital market activity—the legal and regulatory framework and infrastructure are robust, but primary and secondary trading volumes remain low (Bango and Yoon 2024). There is also no covered bond legislation in Kazakhstan, meaning that banks cannot use this instrument for mortgage financing.

Interestingly, Kazakhstan once had a vibrant mortgage securitization market, both domestic and cross-border, with a relevant legal and regulatory framework, active market intermediaries, and strong lender participation. However, since the 2008 global financial crisis, authorities seem to have shifted away from a capital market–oriented ecosystem toward a savings and loan (S&L) housing finance model institutionalized in OTB, which, by design, is not conducive to RMBS issuance.

Kazakhstan's mortgage market landscape, with a significant S&L share and no capital market activity, likely reflects policy decisions taken after the global financial crisis and shaped by the impact of the crisis on Kazakhstani lenders. It incorporates key lessons from the 2008 crisis: avoiding capital market–oriented or adjustable-rate lending, adopting prudent loan-underwriting practices and regulation, and improving the match between mortgage portfolio characteristics and the liabilities used, among others.

TABLE 5.1 Brief history of mortgage securitization in Kazakhstan

YEAR	EVENT
2000	KIK is established by NBK.
2002	KIK carries out domestic issue of mortgage-backed securities (first in CIS).
2006–07	BTA Bank makes cross-border securitization placements.
2013	Shareholder is changed from NBK to Baiterek.
2020	By this year, KIK has purchased over 67,000 mortgages from lenders.
2021	KIK is reorganized into KHC, with a focus on housing construction guarantee and finance.

Source: Original table for this publication.
Note: CIS = Commonwealth of Independent States; KHC = Kazakhstan Housing Company; KIK = Kazakhstan Mortgage Company; NBK = National Bank of Kazakhstan.

However, good global regulatory and policy practices have been adjusted to maintain a balance among various mortgage-funding channels, with particular attention given to mortgage securitization. For example, there have been relevant statutory changes in the European Union and the United States, such as the 2017/2402 EU Securitization Regulation package. There have also been efforts in many countries to severely restrict foreign exchange lending and to discourage intrusive regulatory and legislative attention to securitization practices. Thus, it may be prudent to modernize Kazakhstan's mortgage ecosystem accordingly, specifically by reestablishing a robust and sustainable capital-market-funding channel, as discussed later in chapter 6. The history of mortgage market securitization in Kazakhstan is summarized in table 5.1.

MAIN BENEFITS OF MORTGAGE MARKET–CAPITAL MARKET LINKS

A robust capital market funding and risk management channel for mortgage finance offers several benefits for sector stakeholders:

- It gives lenders access to long-term liabilities to facilitate the origination of long-term mortgage loans, in turn alleviating asset liability management (ALM) pressures and liquidity pressures, even though the cost of such capital may be higher than customers' deposits.
- It can be used by lenders to reduce credit risk, interest rate risk, and market risk, all of which may be transferred to investors in debt securities.[1]
- From a macro perspective, it permits growth of an aggregate mortgage portfolio beyond the banking system's capacity to hold such assets against its capital.
- The robust risk and data disclosure requirements inherent in the mortgage securitization framework provide the regulator with current, detailed, and accurate information about the state of the housing finance market.

- It facilitates deepening of the housing finance market as such, by enabling smaller and less capitalized banks to play a meaningful role in mortgage lending—for example, by performing originator or servicer roles.

At the same time, developing the secondary mortgage market requires significant legal and regulatory effort, a sufficient body of institutional investors, and a certain level of maturity in the general capital market infrastructure and practices. All of these are present in Kazakhstan to a large extent.

Note that globally, mortgage-related capital market practices and instruments vary significantly, in part owing to historical factors and to the overall housing finance configuration. Refer to box 5.1 for the overview of some country examples across the world.

Mortgage securitization via a mortgage market intermediary—potentially an existing institution—may be worth exploring by the Kazakhstani authorities.[2] Given that relevant legal, regulatory, and practical aspects for conveyance of loans and issuance of proper mortgage-backed debt securities are in place, there may be an opportunity to establish a program that assembles pools of market-priced mortgages with similar lending standards for subsequent issuance of market-priced debt instruments.[3] Key benefits of such a program include the potential creation of a viable funding channel for lenders and an additional low-risk investment option for banks and other institutional investors. For Baiterek, a shareholder of KHC—which might be a suitable candidate for such an intermediary entity—an additional motivation would be to establish a funding source for its subsidiary, OTB, thereby reducing funding requirements for the shareholder.

Refinancing—that is, providing long-term secured corporate loans to mortgage lenders for subsequent origination—may also be an option. This is a common mechanism for developing mortgage markets globally (one was used in Kazakhstan in the past) that promotes the market standardization required for robust RMBS issuance. Yet it is significantly less complex than securitization per se. In Kazakhstan, it appears that the required enabling environment is in place, and banks have expressed preliminary interest in obtaining appropriately structured financing to expand their mortgage origination.

It could be helpful to begin by directly exploring lenders' and investors' appetite and preferences, while, in parallel, obtaining a legal opinion on the current enabling framework for mortgage securitization. Issuing securitized paper is a multifaceted undertaking and should thus be approached with due diligence, a thorough understanding of its costs and benefits, and awareness of the institutional capacity needed for regular issuance at meaningful volumes.

Box 5.1

Use of capital market solutions for mortgage finance

Capital market solutions offer mortgage lenders an alternative funding option. They enable them to match the tenor of long-term assets, such as mortgages, with their liabilities, thereby diversifying funding options, transferring credit risk to investors, and, in some instances, freeing up capital to continue lending.

Globally, mortgage lenders utilize capital market instruments in several circumstances:

- Where such a channel is an intrinsic and fundamental feature of the housing finance ecosystem, such as in Canada, Denmark, Mongolia, and the United States.
- Where lenders seek to achieve capital relief and satisfy asset liability management requirements as the share of mortgage loans grows significantly relative to the aggregate credit portfolio, such as in France or Germany.
- Where authorities have institutionalized their housing policy activities by establishing a market intermediary, which supports market development in part by facilitating lenders' access to capital market funding, such as in Japan, Pakistan, and the Russian Federation.

Multiple options exist to provide mortgage-related capital market solutions, and, in more developed markets, several often coexist. Typically, solutions are tailored to the market development stage and evolve from simple to more complex structures as the markets mature. The range of options includes unsecured corporate bonds, covered bonds, and mortgage-backed securities, which could also have some variations.

- Covered bonds are senior debt instruments secured by a pool of mortgage loans to which investors have a preferential claim in the event of an issuer's default. Covered bonds are typically issued by banks and represent a dual-recourse obligation, as investors have recourse against both the issuer and the collateral (the cover pool). They are particularly common in some European countries (for example, France, Germany, and the Nordic countries).
- Residential mortgage-backed securities (RMBS) are debt instruments secured by a dedicated pool of residential mortgage loans. The payments of principal and interest on these securities are funded from the payments of principal and interest made on the underlying mortgage loans by the borrowers. RMBS are issued by a variety of institutions. These include retail financial institutions—for example, banks, nonbank mortgage lenders, and wholesale mortgage aggregators such as secondary mortgage market companies (in Colombia, the Republic of Korea, and Malaysia); they also include specialized government agencies (in Canada and the United States).

The primary mortgage lenders could deploy these options directly or by refinancing their mortgage portfolios through mortgage-refinancing companies (if such institutions are established in a market). Mortgage-refinancing companies could also issue unsecured bonds or mortgage-backed securities to raise long-term funding through the capital markets and pass this funding on to the primary lenders for issuing new mortgage loans.

At the same time, the potential for developing capital market solutions for housing finance in Kazakhstan is mixed. On the one hand, about 70 percent of originations (OTB plus 7-20-25 program loans) are not suited for capital market utilization due to low interest rates. The National Bank of Kazakhstan purchases the 7-20-25 program loans from lenders (via its subsidiary Kazakhstan Stability Fund),[4] but the yield of such loans is materially lower than a prudent investor would expect (7 percent per year versus a likely yield of about 20 percent per year).[5] On the other hand, about 30 percent of mortgage originations have interest rates set on a market basis.[6] Thus, such loans may be considered either for refinancing by a third party for subsequent securitization or for direct issuance of bank-originated debt. The latter option might not be economical due to small per-lender origination volumes,[7] and a multi-originator security issuance or transfer of mortgage pools to a centralized market intermediary might be preferable.

The growth of capital market activities could be impeded by uncertainty about interest rates on both lenders' and investors' sides. As nominal origination volumes remain modest because of high interest rates, lenders may not be interested in expanding their overall mortgage business line or its funding channels. In other words, the currently available liquidity and institutional capacity are sufficient for the number of loans lenders originate. A significant increase in that number is unlikely given banks' eligible clientele. In addition, institutional investors do not have limits on or appetite for mortgage-backed securities, especially without significant prudential and other regulatory preferences. The financial market regulator, in this regard, might consider treating RMBS on a risk basis given sufficient performance data and thus provide for appropriate investor preferences.[8]

Finally, from a policy perspective, it is not inconceivable that two distinct housing finance models coexist within a single jurisdiction. As mortgage lending proper—via second-tier banks—accounts for about a third of the overall housing finance market volume in Kazakhstan, it is reasonable to suggest expanding it. This could be done in part by enabling appropriate funding mechanisms, of which issuance of mortgage-backed securities is a common and potentially readily implementable one.

At the same time, OTB should not be incentivized to dilute its S&L business model to maintain institutional stability. In any S&L institution, there is an inherent origination volume constraint (due to ALM and cash flow–balancing requirements); thus, significant expansion of the housing finance market likely necessitates an increase in mortgage origination beyond OTB. Such growth in conventional mortgages is best supported by the availability of long-term, affordable financial capital from capital markets.

NOTES

1. Actual asset derecognition and removal of risk from lenders require specific transaction terms and conditions and are usually subject to auditor and legal counsel opinion. Modern securitization statutory frameworks, such as the 2017/2402 EU Securitization Regulation package (refer to https://eur-lex.europa.eu/eli/reg/2017/2402/oj/eng), actually require certain levels of lender risk retention in the hope that this will decrease risks of originating low-quality mortgage assets and other undesirable behavior.
2. Securitization is opposed here to refinancing—the extension of corporate loans by a third party to mortgage lenders, who keep the loans on their balance sheet. This modus operandi limits the capital market instrument options to simple corporate debt instead of more complex securitization paper and exerts capital pressure on the issuer.
3. KHC has, in fact, expressed an interest in exploring such activity.
4. The Kazakhstan Stability Fund is an NBK instrument that undertakes financial sector stability and financial support programs. Refer to the fund's website at https://kfu.kz/.
5. This activity illustrates that all needed market infrastructure elements, as well as the legal and regulatory environments, are in place for proper mortgage refinancing.
6. Developer-linked loans have interest rates of about 15 percent, which is below market.
7. In 2024, only two lenders—the Bank Credit Center and Bank Freedom Finance—had significant volumes of originations.
8. The Basel III framework is broadly less favorable to securitization than to mortgage covered bonds—for example, in terms of liquidity coverage ratio and net stable funding ratio inclusion. The sector regulator may have some flexibility, however, to treat local RMBS in a risk-based manner commensurate with actual and expected performance.

REFERENCE

Bango, Zsolt, and Yaewon Yoon. 2024. "Kazakhstan Financial Sector Assessment Program Technical Note: Capital Market Development." Financial Sector Assessment Program, World Bank Group. http://documents.worldbank.org/curated/en/099041124104518186.

6 Vision, SWOT Analysis, and Policy Options

VISION OF A MODERNIZED KAZAKHSTANI MORTGAGE ECOSYSTEM

Earlier chapters addressed the characteristics and limitations of Kazakhstan's current housing finance ecosystem, as well as its divergences from good global practice. This chapter presents a high-level vision of that ecosystem for stakeholders' consideration and as context for the policy options discussed later.

Table 6.1 shows modest affordability of 10–20 percent for products that are not targeted or subsidized. It also shows that subsidies are not available to potential mortgage borrowers from second-tier banks (STBs), except through the National Bank of Kazakhstan's (NBK's) 7-20-25 program, which has been scaled down significantly and is slated for complete closure.

In addition, rows 2 and 3 in table 6.1 indicate untargeted yet subsidized products and illustrate that the current subsidy allocation is significantly suboptimal, as approximately 50 percent of market originations receive budgetary support but do not focus on underserved households (such as lower- and middle-income families, those with informal incomes, first-time homeowners, and young families).

TABLE 6.1 Available housing finance solutions in Kazakhstan

MORTGAGE PRODUCT	LENDER	ELIGIBLE BORROWERS	SUBSIDIZED?	TARGETED?	AFFORDABILITY (%)	MARKET SHARE (%)
Loans under government programs	OTB	Vulnerable, low-income OTB members	Yes	Yes	30–60	15
OTB mortgages	OTB	All OTB S&L members	Yes	No	10–20	45
7-20-25 mortgages	STBs	All	Yes	No	50	5
Regular mortgages	STBs	All	No	No	10–20	35

Sources: Original table for this publication using conversations with stakeholders, OTB, NBK, and STBs.
Note: OTB = Otbasy Bank; S&L = savings and loan; STBs = second-tier banks.

A detailed list of policy options for increasing housing affordability follows. The aim is to deepen the market, increase fiscal efficiency, and enhance private capital participation:

- The targeting and optimization of the savings and loan (S&L) depositor premium could be enhanced. Middle-income members would be targeted both explicitly through means testing and implicitly through tighter criteria for Otbasy Bank (OTB) mortgage product eligibility (for example, by establishing reasonable limits on property price and loan amount that align with market averages). The actual premium amount could, for example, be increased or vary based on depositor income.
- Additional S&L products could be targeted at low-income households or those with informal income, whose savings history would provide a good indicator of their repayment capacity. Mortgage guarantee (MG) protection is frequently utilized with such loans as well. Such a targeted mortgage product could initially be deployed at OTB and subsequently at other STBs, subject to their interest.
- A new down-payment subsidy program could be established and made available to all qualified STBs (criteria to be set by the Agency of the Republic of Kazakhstan for Regulation and Development of Financial Market in consultation with relevant government ministries). The program would involve budget cofinancing of the borrower's down payment and a market-priced loan interest rate. This would allow STBs to participate without decreasing their return on assets through low-yielding mortgage portfolios, and would, at the same time, open the door to a capital-market-funding channel.

While it is not advisable to attempt a broad-based affordability increase via subsidies for the whole market, targeted and judicious use of meaningful subsidies can increase affordability for the population segments that currently cannot afford a mortgage. Table 6.2 presents a high-level vision of how the previously discussed policies would increase the affordability of Kazakhstan's housing finance in the short to medium term, focusing on housing finance products within a 2–3-year horizon.

In the short term, affordability would likely not change significantly—potentially only by 1 decile—mainly because of still-high interest rates. However, the proposed adjustments explicitly target public support toward middle-income, low-income, and first-time homeowners, many of whom could newly qualify for a mortgage loan. The proposed material changes to the housing finance landscape (elaborated in table 6.2) include the following:

- The explicit targeting of all subsidies to address the needs of borrowers with informal, low, or medium incomes, in part via S&Ls' natural strength in enabling long-term savings from such households and supporting their access to subsequent mortgage finance

TABLE 6.2 High-level vision for housing finance products in Kazakhstan, short to medium term

MORTGAGE PRODUCT	LENDER	ELIGIBILITY	SUBSIDIZED?	TARGETED?	AFFORDABILITY (%)	MARKET SHARE (%)
Loans under government programs + mortgage insurance option	OTB (S&L system)	Vulnerable, low-income S&L members	Yes, deposit premium and lower interest rate	Yes	30–60	15
S&L mortgages	S&L system (OTB + STBs)	Middle-income S&L members	Yes, deposit premium	Yes	20–30	25
S&L mortgages + mortgage guarantee option	S&L system (OTB + STBs)	Informal- or low-income S&L members	Yes, deposit premium	Yes	30–40	10
S&L mortgages	S&L system (OTB + STBs)	All S&L members	No	No	10–20	20
Mortgages with down-payment subsidy	STBs	Middle-income borrowers	Yes, down-payment copay	Yes	25–35	10
Regular mortgages + mortgage insurance option	STBs	All	No	No	10–20	20

Source: Original table for this publication using World Bank Group projections.
Note: OTB = Otbasy Bank; S&L = savings and loan; STB = second-tier bank.

- The introduction of a meaningful non-S&L down-payment subsidy to replace interest rate subsidies, which would facilitate subsidized loan liquidity, including for capital market transactions
- The use of mechanisms to mitigate mortgage credit risk, specifically mortgage insurance (MI) and MGs, to improve access to mortgage loans from riskier households.

The estimated market share of the revised mortgage product offering is approximate. Detailed borrower profile data from OTB and other STBs are needed to accurately predict client migration between current and proposed mortgage products.

SWOT MATRIX: OVERALL

With the aim of providing strategic insights to stakeholders, this section presents a high-level review of internal factors (strengths and weaknesses) and external factors (opportunities and threats) in Kazakhstan's housing finance ecosystem. The SWOT (strengths, weaknesses, opportunities, threats) methodology is not the only type of analysis available; complementing it with other approaches is advised.

Strengths (internal)

Strengths in the overall SWOT matrix for Kazakhstan's housing finance ecosystem include the following:

- A well-developed enabling environment and financial infrastructure, including highly digitalized banking processes and products
- An extensive awareness and expertise concerning the housing finance market among public and private stakeholders, as well as robust mortgage-lending products, practices, and systems at major banks
- Large-scale S&L system implementation, with reasonable public support and a strong subsidy transmission component
- A vibrant residential real estate construction sector
- An active banking-industry association.

Weaknesses (internal)

Weaknesses include the following:

- Modest mortgage affordability and concentrated competition for borrowers in the top-two income deciles
- Excessive state involvement in the economy overall and the housing finance sector specifically, potentially limiting competition
- The high cost of financial capital, restricting housing affordability
- A lack of mortgage-backed capital market solutions, restricting long-term capital sources
- A lack of de-risking solutions (such as MG or MI) for market deepening
- Limited room for organic S&L system growth, thus, ceteris paribus, little room to increase affordability via OTB lending alone
- A relatively unseasoned mortgage portfolio and the resulting uncertain nonperforming loan dynamics, especially given the fluid macroeconomic outlook and volatile real estate prices
- Relatively small portfolios at individual lenders, which may limit potential capital-market-financing or -refinancing options
- The intrinsic unsuitability of the largest mortgage portfolio, at OTB, for capital market activities, limiting the potential scale of mortgage-backed issuance
- The likely shallow initial investor appetite for residential mortgage-backed securities, depending on such factors as regulator and market stakeholder support, details of the refinancing model adopted, and so on
- The excess and inefficiency of certain subsidy programs, which can distort the market.

Opportunities (external)

Opportunities include the following:

- The potential for organic portfolio growth outside the S&L system, subject to favorable monetary policy evolutions and lower financial capital cost
- The establishment of a market intermediary and introduction of capital market mortgage-backed instruments to enable lender access to long-term finance
- Market deepening through new mortgage products, such as products for borrowers with informal income or for those seeking Islamic housing finance solutions (which will require significant consumer awareness and protection)
- Subsidy rationalization to improve targeting, increase affordability, reduce fiscal inefficiencies, and support the entry of private financial capital
- The introduction of de-risking solutions such as credit risk guarantees or insurance schemes.

Threats (external)

Threats include the following:

- Fluid regional and global macroeconomic and trade evolutions, which may lead to negative macroeconomic dynamics at the country level, thereby reducing real incomes and introducing unfavorable real estate market dynamics
- Regulatory and policy evolutions that may make it challenging or costly for lenders to maintain or expand their housing finance business line
- Fiscal constraints that may materially reduce government capacity to provide subsidies via OTB and otherwise support mortgage market deepening
- Residential real estate market evolutions that may increase portfolio credit risk for lenders
- Portfolio performance decline, which may put capital consumption pressure on key lenders.

SWOT MATRIX: OTBASY BANK

The following SWOT analysis provides an overview of OTB's strategic position within Kazakhstan's mortgage and housing market. It highlights key internal strengths and weaknesses, as well as external opportunities and threats impacting its operations.

Strengths (internal)

Strengths in the OTB matrix include the following:

- *Exclusive mandate.* OTB is the sole operator of Kazakhstan's housing construction savings system and the designated financial agent for all state housing programs, ensuring a dominant market position.
- *Market leader.* The bank holds over 50 percent of the mortgage market in Kazakhstan, with a loan portfolio exceeding T 3 trillion ~US$5.8 billion and annual disbursements surpassing T 1 trillion (~US$1.9 billion).
- *Stable and low-cost funding model.* The bank relies primarily on long-term customer deposits, supported by state-subsidized bonuses, which provide a stable and inexpensive source of funding.
- *Strong alignment with government policy.* Oversight by Baiterek Holding ensures strategic alignment with Kazakhstan's national housing policy, thereby securing long-term institutional support and stability.
- *Strong profitability and financial resilience.* The bank demonstrated high profitability, with returns on average equity and average assets of 16.6 percent and 2.5 percent, respectively, as of 2025.[1] Regular dividend payouts further reflect its sustainable, cash-generating business model and financial stability.

Weaknesses (internal)

Weaknesses include the following:

- *Narrow focus on housing products.* The bank's activities are limited to housing-related savings and mortgages, and such specialization, albeit by design, reduces stability through macro market and real estate market cycles.
- *Limited accessibility for lower-income groups.* Despite its social mandate, the bank's S&L model tends to benefit middle-income households more than lower-income households, which struggle to accumulate the necessary savings within the required time frame in higher inflationary conditions.
- *Low deposit returns that reduce attractiveness.* Savings products offer below-market returns, which, combined with rising housing prices, diminish the long-term financial appeal for potential OTB depositors.
- *Complex participation requirements.* The phased system (savings accumulation, interim loans, and housing loans) and the need to achieve valuation scores may discourage broader public participation due to perceived complexity.
- *Limited potential for expanding the customer base.* The bank already serves about one-third of the economically active population, and even if rules on subsidy targeting and repeated usage are changed, OTB may not be able to expand the depositor base significantly.

Opportunities (external)

Opportunities include the following:

- *Digital transformation.* Investments in digitalization and process automation could enhance customer experience, improve operational efficiency, and broaden access to financial products.
- *Product innovation.* Developing more flexible or diversified savings and mortgage products could make the bank's offerings more competitive and attract a broader range of customers.
- *Continued government support.* Ongoing alignment with state priorities offers potential for future government-backed programs and policy support that will sustain the bank's strategic importance.

Threats (external)

Threats include the following:

- *Successful monetary policy.* Successful monetary policy can lower the cost of financial capital, thereby increasing competition from private lenders due to lower mortgage interest rates.
- *Government policies.* Changes in government policies, especially in subsidy design or implementation, could negatively affect the bank, particularly its ability to secure funding at below-market rates, either from depositors or the capital market.
- *Potential market competition.* Although currently holding a monopoly in state programs, OTB could face increased competition from commercial banks if regulatory frameworks evolve (specifically easing STBs' access to the housing construction savings system and state subsidies) or market preferences shift.
- *Reputational risk from unmet expectations.* If housing remains unaffordable for key target groups, the public might perceive the bank as less effective in fulfilling its social mandate, which could, in turn, trigger political pressure to reduce fiscal subsidies.
- *Macroeconomic volatility.* Inflation, housing market fluctuations, and changes in macroeconomic policies could negatively impact both the demand for OTB's products and the sustainability of its financial model.
- *Fiscal constraints.* Because the bank's model depends on the deposit subsidy for its attractiveness to members and financial sustainability, any adjustments or delays to subsidy provisions could negatively affect OTB's current business model.

POLICY OPTIONS

The policy options suggested in this section aim to enhance housing affordability while promoting fiscal efficiency of public support programs and mobilizing greater private capital. They focus on better targeting of subsidies to address housing needs for lower- and middle-income families. In parallel, they aim to deepen the private mortgage market by promoting greater competition among mortgage lenders, reestablishing capital-market-funding channels, introducing risk-sharing mechanisms, and developing a regulatory framework for innovative products.

These options are presented in table 6.3 and discussed later in this section.

TABLE 6.3 Policy options to accelerate mortgage market development, mobilize private capital, and enable family investment in housing

OPTION	RESPONSIBLE ENTITY
Strategic and governance reforms	
Establish a clear and coordinated vision for developing the housing finance ecosystem through a sectoral strategy	ARDFM, Baiterek, MIC, MNE, MoF, NBK
Introduce a robust M&E system for public support programs to ensure impact and fiscal efficiency	MIC, MNE, MoF
Conduct a full-scope review of OTB's corporate governance practices	Baiterek, MNE, OTB
Rationalization and targeting of public support	
Review the subsidy system, including its mechanics, targeting, transmission channels, and legal arrangements to improve efficiency of subsidies and strengthen their impact on affordability. For example, • Limit S&L premiums to lower- and middle-income households, and apply means testing. • Adjust S&L deposit and loan pricing to correlate with government bond rates for fiscal efficiency.	ARDFM, MIC, MNE, MoF
Introduce a targeted down-payment support program for lower- and middle-income clients across STBs	MIC, MoF
For all public support options and channels, restrict subsidies to one-time lifetime use per household and impose property transfer limitations	MIC, MNE, MoF
Gradually phase out the 7-20-25 program due to inefficiency and misalignment with NBK's mandate	NBK
Market deepening and innovation	
Reestablish a mortgage-backed capital-market-funding channel, potentially via a refinancing facility	ARDFM, Baiterek, KHC
Introduce mortgage credit risk guarantee and insurance mechanisms to support private lenders and underserved borrowers	ARDFM, Baiterek, KHC
Develop products for borrowers with informal incomes or limited credit histories, leveraging S&L strengths	OTB
Explore Islamic housing finance and related capital market solutions under appropriate regulatory frameworks	ARDFM, STBs
Conduct mortgage portfolio stress tests to manage systemic risk	ARDFM

Source: Original table for this publication.

Note: ARDFM = Agency of the Republic of Kazakhstan for Regulation and Development of Financial Market; Baiterek = Baiterek Holding; KHC = Kazakhstan Housing Company; M&E = monitoring and evaluation; MIC = Ministry of Industry and Construction; MNE = Ministry of National Economy; MoF = Ministry of Finance; NBK = National Bank of Kazakhstan; OTB = Otbasy Bank; S&L = savings and loan; STBs = second-tier banks.

Strategic and governance reforms

Suggested policy options for strategic and governance reforms include the following:

1. Establish a clear and coordinated vision for developing the housing finance ecosystem through a sectoral strategy. When embodied in a sectoral strategy, this vision will serve as a foundation for aligning stakeholders' efforts to ensure an efficient use of public support, engage private sector providers, and introduce a robust impact measurement framework. Designing and implementing a meaningful mortgage market development strategy (for example, as part of the Financial Sector Development Strategy or a national housing strategy) could be done jointly by the financial sector regulator and the government. The options listed below could become coordinated elements of such a strategy.
2. Introduce a robust monitoring and evaluation (M&E) system for public support programs to achieve impact and fiscal efficiency; refer to Melecky et al. (2023) for details. Currently, M&E is rather fragmented and focused on tracking pre-set outputs and intermediate volumes, without assessing socioeconomic impacts (such as affordability) and qualitative aspects (resilience, energy efficiency). This likely incentivizes public institutions to increase their business volume while competing with the private sector. M&E systems for public support programs (and the development finance institutions that administer them, such as Kazakhstan Housing Company and OTB) should aim to measure additionality, fiscal efficiency in addressing market failures, and increased mortgage affordability. Sample impact metrics could include income profiles of subsidy recipients, spatial allocation of mortgages, public-to-private capital cofinancing ratio, effectiveness of the deployed public support, or other suitable outcome indicators.
3. Conduct a full-scope review and reform of OTB's corporate governance practices. A desktop review of OTB's corporate governance highlighted several areas at odds with good global practices. A full-scope assessment of the bank's corporate governance practices should be undertaken to ensure that recommendations are complete, accurate, and based on the effectiveness of actual practices.

Rationalization and targeting of public support

Suggested rationalization and targeting of public support include the following:

1. Conduct a comprehensive analysis of the housing finance subsidies—including their mechanics, targeting, and legal arrangements—to strengthen their impact on affordability. The issue of subsidies and their efficient use is especially relevant given the recent exclusion from the state budget of OTB depositor premium contributions (and, by extension, S&L depositor premium contributions; refer to box 4.2. for details). Given the limited

information available at this point, it is challenging to outline OTB-specific areas of such reform. However, it is likely that material adjustments to the mechanics and targeting of savings premium subsidies, along with related legal arrangements, need to be considered. In addition, OTB's management and shareholders will likely need to consider significant adjustments to the bank's business model and financial performance expectations. This analysis and potential adjustments to the S&L system should ideally be part of the comprehensive strategic approach to Kazakhstan's housing finance sector. Among the issues to consider are these:

- *Limiting S&L premiums to lower- and middle-income households and applying means testing, together with product design and eligibility criteria such as loan amount or house price maxima.*[2] Currently, the down-payment subsidy benefits all members regardless of their income and chosen mortgage products, some of which allow for very high loan amounts and are affordable by only the top 10 percent of families by income.[3] Socially vulnerable households targeted under public programs, as well as first-time homebuyers, should continue to receive the premiums on their S&L savings. Once properly focused, premium levels may be adjusted upward to provide meaningful support to eligible depositors on their path to homeownership.
- *Adjusting S&L deposit and loan pricing to correlate with government Treasury bills and bond rates for fiscal efficiency.* The S&L deposit and loan pricings are currently fixed at 2 percent and 5 percent, respectively. Periodic adjustments to track relevant government debt rates, as Germany does, could help protect the government budget and increase fiscal efficiency. Any such transition should not affect current OTB depositors. Although the rates will change over time in line with monetary policy, they will also be fixed at contract signing, so the depositor should have clarity on both the deposit rate and the potential loan interest rate.

2. Introduce a targeted down-payment support program for lower- and middle-income clients across STBs.[4] This should help increase private sector market participation and improve subsidy efficiency. A down-payment subsidy (in the form of a deposit premium) is currently exclusive to OTB S&L depositors. However, down-payment support need not be exclusive to the S&L system, in general, or to OTB, in particular. Specifically, a down-payment subsidy could take the form of a copay from public resources that matches the borrower's contribution (for example, up to 15 percent of the property price). This effective doubling of the borrower's down payment reduces the loan amount and monthly payments, increasing affordability. Such a mechanism also has a significant public-to-private capital multiplier, as mortgage loans can be provided by STBs.[5] In addition, mortgages at market rates with subsidized down payments (as compared to loans at subsidized below-market rates) are more liquid—that is, lenders can transfer or securitize them without discounting their price or requiring additional budget subsidies.

3. Restrict subsidies to once-in-a-lifetime use and impose property transfer limitations for all public support options and channels. Currently, borrowers can obtain a loan from the OTB S&L system more than once.[6] Given their savings and monthly repayment capacity, borrowers with higher incomes can benefit from down-payment support disproportionally more. Other forms of public housing finance support should also be extended only once per household. In addition, consideration should be given to restricting, for a reasonable period, any transfer of property obtained with subsidized mortgages.
4. Gradually phase out the 7-20-25 program considering its inefficiency and misalignment with the NBK mandate. Following its recent downsizing, the program's yearly volume is T 100 billion (~US$195 million), or 5 percent of the recent total of yearly originations; thus, the program is relatively small, loosely targeted, fiscally inefficient, and, importantly, at odds with the stated NBK mandate.[7]

Market deepening and innovation

Suggested policy options for market deepening and innovation include the following:

1. Reestablish a mortgage-backed capital-market-funding channel, potentially via a refinancing facility. This may be a straightforward undertaking, given that the relevant legal and regulatory framework is well-developed and stakeholders have experience. This step could be followed by securitization (by a refinancing facility or individual banks) and the introduction of covered bonds. Harmonization of servicing and special servicing practices may help reduce credit and reputational risks and maintain high levels of consumer protection. Although such a transition will likely benefit major private lenders (and not OTB, given its low-yielding portfolio), the overall impact on affordability and market development could be significant, considering the potential influx of capital.
2. Introduce mortgage credit risk guarantee or insurance mechanisms to support private lenders and underserved borrowers. This market infrastructure can promote market deepening primarily for private lenders, who are likely unfamiliar with borrowers in the middle-income segment of the market or those with informal income. Standard MI may provide down-payment support and be a highly efficient subsidy mechanism for young families or others without a significant down payment, while MGs may facilitate market deepening toward borrowers with low and informal incomes. MGs are a highly efficient mechanism for subsidy transmission to lower-income and informal-income families and socially vulnerable borrowers.
3. Provide S&L mortgage products designed for borrowers with informal incomes or limited credit histories. The S&L system by its nature supports borrowers with undocumented or informal incomes or without a credit history. It becomes even more supportive when coupled with a credit risk

protection mechanism, such as an MG, which can itself be an efficient subsidy transmission channel and increase fiscal effectiveness while mobilizing private capital in tandem.

4. Explore Islamic housing finance and related capital market solutions under appropriate regulatory frameworks, such as with respect to consumer awareness and protection. A robust analysis of market demand and the impact on affordability should be undertaken before implementing any of these solutions.

5. Conduct mortgage portfolio stress tests to manage systemic risk. Given uncertain near-term macroeconomic dynamics, such stress tests could be used to assess potential capital consumption and social impact under plausible worst-case scenarios. Developer-linked mortgage loans could pose elevated levels of risk and require attention from the banking supervisor. Notably, mortgage portfolio analytical methods and conventions should be standardized across the industry, and key results and data should be periodically published—especially to support efforts to develop capital-market-funding activities—for the benefit of the investor and analyst community. Mortgage market reform in Kazakhstan is a strategic priority to expand housing affordability, improve fiscal efficiency, and mobilize private capital. Stakeholders—the government, regulators, financial institutions, and development partners—must act jointly to design and implement a coordinated housing finance strategy. Such a strategy is essential for aligning efforts; ensuring efficient use of public resources; and building an inclusive, resilient mortgage ecosystem that meets the needs of Kazakhstan's growing economy and diverse population.

NOTES

1. OTB unaudited financial statements as of December 31, 2025.
2. For example, the property price maximum as appraised by a licensed independent valuer can be set at the national average selling price for the previous year (or a practical shorter time period). This would incentivize more transactions outside the major metropolitan statistical areas, as well as likely reducing the motivation of families in top income deciles to use S&L facilities.
3. Loan amounts reach up to T 100 million (~US$195,000), while the average OTB loan amount is T 15 million (~US$29,000).
4. A subsidy down-payment copay increases borrower equity and reduces the loan amount, so that, even in the context of high interest rates, periodic mortgage payments are reduced to accommodate household incomes. This approach increases affordability without sacrificing mortgage loan liquidity (because the interest rate is market priced) and makes the loan suitable for capital market use.
5. This effect depends on the exact mechanics—for example, budgetary down-payment support that matches borrower savings would have affordability impact equal to or better than a nominally low interest rate.
6. By contrast, the NBK 7-20-25 program explicitly limits program eligibility to once per lifetime.
7. The program carries an annual mortgage interest rate of 7 percent compared with about 20 percent from banks.

REFERENCE

Melecky, Martin, Pasquale Di Benedetta, Ismael Ahmad Fontan, Ganbaatar Jambal, and Michel Noel. 2023. *Braced for Impact: Reforming Kazakhstan's National Financial Holding for Development Effectiveness and Market Creation.* World Bank Group. https://openknowledge.worldbank.org/entities/publication/afbb7e36-ad92-4205-9b91-715eb4bd00e8.

APPENDIX A

List of stakeholders interviewed

The following list includes stakeholders who were interviewed or responded to written questionnaires or data requests during the preparation of this report.

PUBLIC SECTOR STAKEHOLDERS
Agency for Protection and Development of Competition
Agency of the Republic of Kazakhstan for Regulation and Development of Financial Market
Kazakhstan Housing Company
Ministry of Industry and Construction
National Bank of Kazakhstan
National Managing Holding "Baiterek"
Otbasy Bank
PRIVATE SECTOR STAKEHOLDERS
Association of Financiers of Kazakhstan
Center Credit Bank
Freedom Bank
Halyk Bank